VICTORIAN BOTTLES
A Collector's Guide to Yesterday's Empties

John Stockton

David & Charles
Newton Abbot   London   North Pomfret (Vt)

To my father-in-law Clifford Evans

British Library Cataloguing in Publication Data

Stockton, John
   Victorian bottles.
    1. Bottles – England – Collectors and collecting
    I. Title   II. Stockton, Norman
    748.8   NK5440.B6
   ISBN 0–7153–8141–5

Library of Congress Catalog Card Number 80-85499

Filmset in Monophoto Baskerville by
Latimer Trend & Company Ltd, Plymouth
and printed in Great Britain by
Butler & Tanner Limited, Frome
for David & Charles (Publishers) Limited
Brunel House Newton Abbot Devon

Published in the United States of America
by David & Charles Inc
North Pomfret Vermont 05053 USA

CONTENTS

ACKNOWLEDGEMENTS

I would like to thank all those who have helped in any way in the research and compilation of this book. In particular my wife, Megan, and children, Claire, Jonathan and Simon, for their patience and understanding; fellow authors, John Doxat, Les Martin and Brian Spiller, for timely advice, help and encouragement; Colin Packham for photographs from the Dewar, Haddon and Martin collections of whisky jugs; Arthur Lycett and Mike Pritchard for photographic assistance; the following organisations for their generous co-operation: Allied Services Limited; J. & E. Atkinson Limited; Beecham Group Limited; Arthur Bell & Sons Limited; Bolton Museum & Art Gallery; Boots Company Limited; Bovril Limited; Buchanan Booth's Agencies Limited; James Buchanan & Company Limited; Cadbury Schweppes Limited; Chesebrough-Pond's Limited; Colman Foods; Coates & Company (Plymouth) Limited; Coca-Cola Company; C.P.C. (United Kingdom) Limited; Crosse & Blackwell Limited; Dairy Trade Federation; Denby Tableware Limited; John Dewar & Sons Limited; Distillers Company Limited; Doulton & Company Limited; Eldridge, Pope & Company Limited; Express Dairy Group Services Limited; Fortnum & Mason Limited; J. S. Fry & Company Limited; Glass Manufacturers Federation; Arthur Guinness, Son & Company (Dublin) Limited; John Haig & Company Limited; Hammonds Sauce Company Limited; Harrods Limited; John Harvey & Sons Limited; James Keiller & Son Limited; Lea & Perrins Limited; Marks & Spencer Limited; Milk Marketing Board; Old Bushmills Distillery Company; Parker Pen Company Limited; Patent Office, Orpington; R. Paterson & Sons Limited; Pearson & Company (Chesterfield) Limited; J. R. Phillips & Company Limited; Pilkington Glass; Redfearn National Glass Limited; James Robertson & Sons Limited; Sanitas Company Limited; Seagram United Kingdom Limited; Gordon Tanqueray & Company Limited; William Teacher & Sons Limited; John Walker & Sons Limited; Watneys London Limited; Whitbread & Company Limited; Yardley & Company Limited.

PREFACE

My aim in writing this book on Victorian bottles is to be both entertaining and discursive. Its appeal, therefore, may hopefully extend beyond the enthusiasm of antique bottle collectors and prospective collectors to a wider reading public, and embrace some aspect of validity for all who love our yesterdays and appreciate the craftsmanship and vitality of a society at its zealous best.

The subject is fascinating in many ways, but it is mainly through bottles and jars that the book examines some of the developments of the Victorians at their most vigorous and enterprising period. It studies entrepreneurial advancements, provides insight into the struggles of the small businessman, and looks at advertising techniques, cut-price warfare, industrial espionage, mergers, takeovers and the growth of some of today's giants. It takes us through that shifting curtain and links us with the past.

It is also my intention that the book should be of practical use to those wishing to become collectors of antique bottles, for it considers typical collectors' items which can be found in river beds, canals, mines, ravines, quarries, gravel and chalk pits, marl-holes, brick-fields, marshlands and isolated communities. It attempts to understand the irony of the fact that the Victorian housewife treated empty household containers with the same disregard her modern counterpart has for plasticated vessels, and suggests why possibly the most lucrative period as far as bottle collectors are concerned dates from 1880 to 1900.

Should the book develop the purpose of practical knowledge and give it a deeper significance by illustrating how potters and glassmakers achieved their end products and how those products were exploited, then I feel it will have succeeded in providing a worthwhile and reliable insight into the significant role played by the glass and earthenware bottle in Victorian society.

John Stockton 1981

1
VICTORIAN RUBBISH DUMPS

In order to appreciate more fully why the last two decades of the nineteenth century provided us with such a legacy of 'rubbish', it might be useful to examine briefly the social and economic developments in communications, industry, and particularly in public health and hygiene, which led up to this period.

As with any industrial development, were it in glassware, earthenware, or indeed any large sector of industry, the question of transport was vital. Roads, for example, did not begin to benefit from experiments in worthwhile drainage and surfacing until the middle of the eighteenth century and travel costs were high. By the turn of the century, however, there had been a marked increase in the volume of manufactured goods, and canals played a vital role in supply and demand for both raw materials and finished products.

In order to increase productivity, more and more people were drawn into the industrial areas where the expanding labour force naturally demanded to be fed. This in turn necessitated improvement and expansion not only in agricultural methods but also in glass and earthenware container production. Initially, the glass and pottery producing areas had had to rely on wide-wheeled eight-ton road waggons, each drawn by a team of twelve horses, to transport their wares over any real distance, but such vehicles proved slow and cumbersome. Enterprising manufacturers like Josiah Wedgwood found both the pack-horse system and these lumbering waggons irksome in the extreme. Ships, for example, bringing important raw materials such as kaolin from Cornwall were speedy enough, but once unloaded at Runcorn the ball-clay had to be transported overland to the Potteries by pack-horse, which was exceedingly slow. Breakages, too, were frequent in the despatch of finished goods for obvious reasons, and the

Victorian working-class houses in close proximity to a potbank, Stoke-on-Trent
(Courtesy Albion Galleries)

producers of glass containers were faced with similar problems.

The potters and many like them who had previously invested money in turnpike roads, now began to turn their attention to canals as a speedier and more lucrative mode of communication. Beginning with Bridgewater's canal in 1761 these 'arteries of the revolution' (as Hadfield calls them) were quickly seized upon by entrepreneurs like Earl Gower, Wedgwood, Bentley and the Cheshire salt manufacturers. A network of canals had been constructed by 1800 to transport food and raw materials into industrial regions on a much larger scale than before, and it was now possible to distribute manufactured goods in greater bulk and with greater safety throughout the kingdom. The Victorian age, incidentally, saw the running of fly-boats, an important time-tabled service which relied on double crews and relays of horses to maintain a comparatively quick and efficient merchandise and parcels service. Passenger-carrying canal-boats, too, were still popular in the 1830s and 1840s, being far superior in comfort and cleanliness to stage coaches and other forms of road transport. The irony was, of course, that in late Victorian times these narrow-boats together with their often very picturesque canals should become the 'wet roadways' so prominent in great rubbish disposal schemes.

The economic decline of canals in Britain was inevitable, however, with the onset of the railway mania of the 1840s. Their lack of uniformity was soon taken advantage of by the speedier, more punctual and more convenient railway network which was (unlike the canal system) quick to consolidate under men like George Hudson. The growth of State control tended to strengthen railway domination in that it brought about uniformity of gauge, imposed maximum rates for carriage of goods, and adjudicated over disputes between companies. The railways were essential to a healthy Victorian economy, particularly in the later years when they became (collectively) one of Britain's major employers. They also considerably reduced transport costs and brought coal and other important raw materials cheaply and efficiently to manufacturing districts on a far greater scale than did canals. They were paramount in extending the factory system through-out the United Kingdom by their ability to transport finished products quickly, safely and in bulk, thus creating the sizeable markets so essential to successful industrialisation.

By 1851, Britain had become known as the workshop of the world, and displayed her material prosperity at the Great Exhibition of that year in Joseph Paxton's Crystal Palace, built at first in London's Hyde Park. The building, like the new mechanised age it symbolised, was revolutionary in every way: it was a huge greenhouse of iron and glass, utterly unlike the conventional architecture of the period not only in visual impact but also in its designer's innovative use of prefabrication. This new method, whereby the iron columns, girders, roof-trusses, gutters, frames for the glass and the 400 tons of glass itself, all arrived on site ready-made, was so progressive in planning and facilitated such an unprecedented speed of construction, that it set the trend for an exhibition which was to astound the world with its ingenuity and futuristic impact. Raw materials, machinery, manufactures and fine arts were all indicative of the impressive industrial achievement of the first half of the nineteenth century. Locomotives, marine engines, giant looms, cranes, hydraulic presses, agricultural equipment, textiles, the latest fashions in furniture and hardware – the latter section including early water-closets, a refrigerator and a gas cooker – all served to excite the thousands of visitors who paid either 1s (5p), 2s 6d (12½p), 5s (25p) or £1 admission according to the day of the week on which they attended. A great many of the leading pottery and glass-ware manufacturers exhibited a profusion of intricate designs and decorations, whilst it should not go unmentioned that the plate-glass manufacturers supplied the 300,000 panes for the roof and walls of Paxton's Palace. Thus the amenities of life were in some measure seen to be increasing for all. Humanitarianism, however, had not kept pace with industrial excellence, for beneath the polished surface of peace and prosperity there still lurked ignorance, poverty and degradation. Many large manufacturing towns had indeed degenerated through squalor, for there were no regulations covering planning, water supplies, sewage disposal and the like.

When Victoria became queen in 1837 the average life expectancy of a working man was between thirty-nine and forty years. In those days, of course, few people connected epidemic diseases with squalid conditions although some measures were in fact being taken to improve water supplies, social hygiene and medicines. Despite this, however, the early years of Victoria's reign saw a dramatic rise in the death rate. In retrospect it can be said that overcrowding in large factory towns was a major contributory factor. Living conditions, particularly ventilation and sanitation, were atrocious. Piped water supplies were almost unheard of, as was refuse disposal, although throughout the 1850s and 1860s there was some effort to remove cesspools and provide water-closets and dustbins for the 'houses of the superior classes'. Open sewers for surface drainage were in general use, and as both cholera and typhoid were water-borne diseases, thousands died between 1830 and 1870. Cholera found its way to England in the nineteenth century from India, a severe outbreak in 1849 causing the deaths of 14,000 people in London alone. The disease was caused by a bacterium in the stomach and intestines, but it was not until 1866 that it was established that cholera was spread by flies and contaminated water supplies. Typhus or ship's fever on the other hand was spread by lice, and thrived in the overcrowded and disgusting conditions of early Victorian England.

The distribution of water to what the social reformer Edwin Chadwick called the 'wage classes' was by company-owned standpipes which were perhaps turned on for an hour or two each day. Butter tubs were utilised to store water in living rooms, washing water being used over and over again. Entire courts and streets were often served by a single over-flowing privy, and because there were no facilities for the disposal of rubbish or slops, the stink of filth and decay between the tight-packed back-to-back houses was overwhelming. Men like Henry Doulton, however, were striving for a solution and by 1846 the Lambeth factory was in the vanguard of the revolution in sanitation which Chadwick and the great reformers of the day brought to metropolitan England.

A concerted effort was made at this time to replace the cesspool system with house drainage, but lack of proper supervision frequently resulted in inefficient workmanship and therefore defective sewer linkage to houses. Many dwellings were actually built over rubbish tips, particularly in areas scheduled for massive land reclamation, but it wasn't until 1879 that builders were forced by law to seal over the refuse with concrete. This supposedly provided a 'float' between the buildings and the dump, although the foundations were often cheaply mixed and soon cracked to allow germs to pervade the premises above.

In the larger towns and cities some ash-pits and dustbins were provided, but being so few in number in relation to the population, they were of no real value in the struggle against disease. Bad fish, meat and vegetables were still regularly thrown into open dust-holes and left to decompose, whilst unoccupied rooms and cellars were used as depositories for more rotting garbage. Many tenement houses still had only a single water supply, but even in areas where houses boasted individual supplies, they probably came from unprotected cisterns and were more than likely to have been used for both flushing sewerage and drinking.

Water-closets were in use in most built-up areas by 1887, the Queen's Golden Jubilee Year, although again not in sufficient numbers to prove worthwhile. Some districts had only one closet between a dozen or more houses. Consequently, make-shift appliances found their way into cellars, often being allowed to overflow for months on end. These cellars

Sewage spilling into River Fleet, London, *c* 1845 (*Line drawing by Norman Stockton*)

were frequently used by the homeless as places to sleep, the filth and stench apparently being preferable to no roof at all.

Britain's geographical position, and the fact that a high percentage of her income from overseas territories took the form of imported raw materials, made her particularly vulnerable to epidemic diseases through her shipping lines. Asiatic cholera, an acute form characterised by violent diarrhoea, cramps, and a high death rate, was most common in India towards the end of the nineteenth century and thus posed a very real threat to these islands. The shortest route from the East to Europe was, of course, the Suez Canal in which Disraeli, in 1875, had acquired almost a half share for Britain at a cost of £4 million. Because of its considerable usage by British shipping in the 1880s, fears arose that cholera, prevalent in North Africa in 1883, might spread to the British Isles, inducing many local government authorities to advise inhabitants of densely populated areas as to the precautions they might take. Handbills usually included the following advice:

Diarrhoea –	seek medical treatment immediately.
Disinfectants –	thoroughly disinfect sinks and water-closets with carbolic acid.
Drainage & Refuse –	empty water-closets frequently and free all blocked drains. Burn all vegetable refuse.
Dustbins –	do not allow dustbins to overflow.
Sinks –	flush sinks daily with water, and keep on sink covers.
Ventilation –	keep houses clean and well ventilated, especially bedrooms.
Water-supply –	make certain all water-butts are clean, and report immediately any possible infiltration of the water-closet by dirty water or a defective supply.

Carbolic acid, in its pure state consisting of colourless, needle-shaped crystals, was a powerful and penetrating antiseptic and a strong disinfectant. It could be obtained free by the poor in most towns and cities when epidemic threatened.

The death of Queen Victoria's husband, Albert, from typhoid in 1861 had made it clear that the disease knew no social barriers. But when his son, the Prince of Wales, became infected ten years later, pressures for reform brought about the much needed Public Health Acts of the 1870s. The authorities were compelled to take action against infectious diseases and, among other things, to maintain sewers. The provision of water supplies, baths and wash-houses were also recommended but not obligatory. Chadwick's earlier report on the sanitary state of the working classes equated the high cost of poor relief with social squalor and recommended that the most important and practicable measures to improve conditions should be drainage, the betterment of water supplies, and the removal of all refuse from habitations, streets and roads. Attempts were made, but the implementation of the latter of these recommendations in large cities found an obstacle in the considerable expense of hand labour and cartage. Not being borne by the rates as today, the cost of refuse disposal had to come from the re-cycling of rubbish.

Marl-hole dump with scavengers, Potteries, c 1900 (*Courtesy Albion Galleries*)

Many towns and cities made considerable profits from refuse collection initially, and large open dust-carts drawn by nose-bagged horses and attended by men with leather flaps at the back of their hats collected rubbish daily for corporation storage centres. Here adults and children, known as scavengers, would sort through piles of putrefying garbage salvaging any item which could be sold. Bottles, of course, were purchased by breweries and bottling plants, whilst glass and pottery fragments were in demand for the foundations of buildings and roadways. They were also used in the making of bricks, and old abandoned brickworks sometimes conceal prolific hoards of bottles. They would have been taken there, crushed, and added to the raw clay. New techniques introduced before the turn of the century, however, rendered the process obsolete and many bottles were left for a hundred years, the passage of time digging their graves beneath nettles and brambles.

Improved methods had considerably lessened production costs in the glass and wool industries which, until the 1870s, had been among the main patrons of corporation refuse centres. Within ten years scavenging had been abandoned and unsorted rubbish containing a fascinating assortment of Victorian bottles and jars began to be dumped on marshlands, in marl-holes and worked-out quarries, and indeed any such area accessible by rail or canal. Unfortunately, the end of

13

Partly exposed late nineteenth-century rubbish dump, Newcastle-under-Lyme. Note the nettles, cinders and fragments of glass and pottery (*Author's collection*)

Victoria's reign saw the decline of lengthy transport operations as the great Edwardian cities began to adopt incineration as the long-term answer to the disposal of garbage, thus diminishing the scope of twentieth-century collectors of Victoriana.

In spite of the trend away from dumping, and for various other reasons, bottles and jars of the late nineteenth century found their way into all kinds of unlikely places. Thousands of beer and spirit bottles, for example, were used as ballast in the holds of prison ships bound for Australia. Troops strung out across a vast British Empire received

14

regular supplies of products which remain household names today: Bovril, Camp Coffee, Worcestershire Sauce, and numerous well-known brands of whiskies and beers. At home, huge quantities of glass and earthenware containers had already been emptied of their contents in the normal course of domestic routine and relegated to the local dump. These dumps differed considerably from region to region and were often determined not only by population density and industry but also by the terrain.

In country districts, people were left to their own devices with regard to rubbish disposal until well into the twentieth century. Usually in outlying areas houses were built from local materials, and many stone and slate quarries later provided excellent receptacles for unwanted refuse. Old people living in such areas can often still remember such sites being used in their early childhood or are at least aware of them through knowledge handed down. On the very isolated farmsteads and cottages, the occupants would select sites away from buildings and good workable land. Hedgerows occasionally reveal assortments of bottles in their root systems as do bramble thickets, copses and nettle beds. Woodland ravines and cart-tracks built over uneven or marshy ground also provided possible dumping places.

In the towns where refuse was officially collected but no longer sorted out it was transported, usually by cart or narrow-boat, to dumps well beyond the limits of densely populated areas. The 'canal mania' of the early 1790s in particular had provided a network of inland waterways from the Thames to the Humber and these were to furnish many industrial areas with a cheap and easy form of transportation for their unwanted rubbish. Mostly speculative investments in an atmosphere of laissez-faire, these waterways were usually intended to exploit local requirements. Few would have envisaged their use as garbage pipelines a century later, but the canals not only had the advantage of penetrating the very centres of manufacture, towns and cities, they also provided convenient man-made dumping grounds along their routes. Canals required an impervious lining, and it is well known that this was obtained by a method known as puddling. Clay and sand were mixed together to form a water-tight lining and thus numerous clay and sand pits came into being within close proximity of the waterways. Having served their initial purpose, these pits were obvious sitings for waste materials in Victorian times, being easy to reach and capable of absorbing large quantities of garbage over a period of years. Indeed, many were allowed to settle and were then re-used. Thus containers spanning some ten or twenty years may be found in the same dump, provided digging is undertaken sensibly and thoroughly.

Cauldon Canal, near Leek, with narrow-boat – a refuse 'pipeline' (Author's collection)

Serious bottle collectors, of course, have their own methods of identifying dumps, but perhaps the obvious approach is to scour the Victorian archives of libraries in the area intended for exploration. Patience and a great deal of hard searching will, more often than not, reveal clues to the location of dumps and these can be followed up with the use of ordnance survey maps to pin-point accurate sitings. But the spotting of these is mainly common sense, for materials such as coal, clay, chalk, gravel, sand and limestone have been gouged out of the earth from well before the dawn of the industrial revolution. These huge artificial dustbins proved the ideal answer to a refuse disposal problem which faced many authorities towards the end of the 1880s and were usually given some form of coverage by the local press.

The astute observer, should he have taken the trouble to get to know an area fairly well, will be looking for tell-tale signs of his own regarding the source of well-hidden 'treasure'. Because the majority of dumps were comprised for the most part of cinders and ashes, certain types of flora tend to thrive in areas where large deposits of these lie buried. Nettles in particular grow profusely on patches of waste land such as this, as do elders and blackthorn. Pottery and glass fragments lying on the surface of sites or between the roots of bushes or small trees in such areas are often indicative of more lucrative finds below. Farmers ploughing such tracts sometimes unearth small clues to the possible whereabouts of dumps, and building sites tend to be even more revealing. The burrowings of foxes, rabbits and badgers in country districts, too, occasionally bring to light hiding places of bottles worth hundreds of pounds. The loose-packed earth of most dumps is ideal for burrowing animals and also easily probed, the metal rod of the enthusiastic collector informing him of the glass below the surface. The composition of glass fragments will, in most cases, provide reasonable evidence as to the age of a dump.

The majority of containers found in dumps would, at least prior to the 1860s, probably have come from the better off type of home, for until this time the working classes could ill afford to throw anything away. Most were unable to satisfy their primary needs as far as food was concerned without maximum family effort – both parents and as many children as possible working. We must bear in mind here, of course, that the education and leisure necessary for the cultural improvement of the working classes were not forthcoming until very late in the nineteenth century. Thus, a situation prevailed whereby the proletariat bought foodstuffs and other domestic commodities at the stalls of local markets where traders would measure out the small quantities required, often re-filling bottles and jars brought specifically for that purpose. If anything at all was thrown away from these extremely humble dwellings it would have been of little value – ashes, no-deposit bottles and the broken stems and bowls of cheap clay pipes.

The middle classes on the other hand, riding the crest of industrial prosperity, bought much and threw away plenty. These richer house-holds with their servants and lavish entertainings drew upon a wealth of merchandise, and the refuse of affluence would almost certainly have included perfume bottles with ornate stoppers, pickles and preserve jars in varying shades of green glass, earthenware blacking pots, ink pots, pale blue sauce bottles and a fascinating assortment of cosmetic pots and jars, many with beautifully decorated lids.

Not all valuable pieces are found in the big dumps, however, for a goodly number of worthwhile items come to light in cellars, attics and out-houses of neglected town and country dwellings. The abandoned lock-keeper's or game-keeper's cottage, usually well away from the beaten track, will sometimes reveal the most prolific finds. Gardens of such habitations have probably long since been reclaimed by wilderness, but a methodical search will almost certainly produce traces of some once handy site for the dumping of unrequired household rubbish. Refuse from these isolated abodes had to go somewhere, remember, and it couldn't all be burnt.

The Victorian age was a paradise for 'quacks' and some form of cure-all would have found its way into most households, for even hardy country folk must have suffered a small degree of family illness. Once emptied, these bottles would probably have been submerged along with the daily ashes in some remote corner of the garden close to a hedge. Many would certainly have been buried no more than three or four spades deep. Ashes and cinders were also sometimes used by small-holders in outlying districts to reinforce cartways or to encourage nettles and such like to grow in chicken-runs, and this is worth bearing in mind when making a search.

Even the ruined foundations of dwellings are worthy of exploration, as the keen eye can soon trace the original layout of a garden or out-house, even in the height of summer when everything is overgrown. Old country buildings are a must for the bottle enthusiast and often reveal specimens that have lain, totally ignored by the occupants, in the same place for years. Farm out-buildings are a good example of this, for cavities where timbered joists rest on sandstone blocks provide ideal lodgings for bottles which once contained animal medicines – Day's 'Black Drink', a stimulant for calves, lambs, horses and cattle; Elliman's 'Royal Embrocation for Horses'; or Luddington's Oils for cattle.

Cellars of old pubs, frequently situated in city areas due for redevelopment, can unburden hordes of antique beer and spirit bottles, some, if you are very lucky, still retaining their original contents, closures and labels. Lofts in out-houses of country pubs, too, are sometimes worth a look, although the main interest for collectors in some such hostelries is the publican's personal collection of bottles (antique and otherwise) displayed behind the bar.

The current interest in canals as places of recreation also provides the collector with ample opportunity for salvaging Victorian bottles. Where a lock or section of waterway is under repair, a careful probing of the exposed mud-covered bed can often reveal glass and earthenware containers long since discarded by bargees or perhaps by trippers on 'wakes' outings from the nearest large towns. Another likely dumping place for bottles is where canals pass through industrial areas. Here factory hands could purchase for one penny each ginger beers or soda waters to drink with their 'snapping'. Any no-deposit containers were then probably hastily thrown in the water as the firm's bell sounded a return to work. Many canal spurs, particularly in densely populated areas, have been closed down, drained and partially filled in, and here again a detailed search amid rushes, weeds and under top-soil may unearth the odd container cast aside over a century ago.

Such bottles, having lain for so long in adverse conditions, often defy all efforts to restore them to their original state. Water, for example, will erode the lime and soda content in glass, resulting in iridescence. Such discolourations are thought by some collectors to be extremely attractive, and bottles affected in this way are considered valuable and should therefore not be cleaned in the usual manner. Another possible side-effect of glass bottles having been buried over a long period of time in (say) mud is opalescence, which takes the form of a milky-bluish coating on the glass. This is known as 'sick' glass and again is considered an added attraction in a bottle's features, especially by collectors in the United States. To attempt to remove this scale could thus devalue a bottle's worth considerably.

As well as the conventional bottles and jars found in Victorian dumps (be they the large corporation sites or the corners of country vegetable patches), a rich and sought-after collection of ancillary items can be uncovered. Articles well worth retaining include baby-feeders, stone-ware hot water bottles, dolls heads, pocket spitoons (probably minus their pewter lids), figurines, glass fire extinguishers, fairy lights, milk glassware, pot lids, bottle closures and clay pipes. Broken clay pipes, incidentally, can be mended so perfectly by collectors that it is difficult to detect that bowl and stem were once severed. Made from kaolin, a fine white clay formed by the decomposition and weathering of felspar in granite and found extensively in Cornwall, their composition can conveniently be simulated by modern materials and remarkable restoration achieved.

All containers recovered from dumps, be they earthenware or glass, should not be cleaned or exposed to normal conditions right away. A period of between two and three days is recommended to allow containers time to adjust to climatic conditions above ground and so prevent cracking. When a suitable period of time has elapsed, bottles should be superficially cleaned to remove loose dirt and then washed in a solution of soda and luke-warm water. Stubborn stains can usually be eradicated by applying a small quantity of fine gravel or sand mixed with water to the inside of the vessel and swirling it round. The immersion and rotation of a bottle in a bucket of fine sand can have a similar result regarding its exterior. A final polish with cerium oxide will produce a permanent shine well worthy of a display shelf.

2

EARTHENWARE AND GLASS PRODUCTION

It was not until the 1760s that earthenware bottles for wines and ales were made in any quantity in England. Previously they had been imported from Germany, though the 1690s saw the establishing of kilns at Fulham by the potter John Dwight, where the making of stoneware in its true vitrified form was brought to a high degree of perfection. Other potbanks were soon opened at Lambeth, Derby, Nottingham and Chesterfield, and gradually the bottle trade from Europe was effectively diminished. Indeed for the next two hundred years English pottery manufacturers proved formidable competitors to their glass-making counterparts as providers of a variety of containers for foodstuffs and liquids.

A large percentage of these earthenware containers were initially produced by the Lambeth group of potteries, which included the firm of Doulton & Co who were trading in 1815 from Vauxhall Walk as Jones, Watts & Doulton. Recently out of apprenticeship, John Doulton was taken into partnership by Martha Jones, who had inherited the pottery from her late husband. Her foreman, John Watts, was also made a partner, and so began the long and distinguished history of a company synonymous with ceramics throughout the world – Royal Doulton.

Possibly the largest pottery manufacturer outside London during Victoria's reign was Joseph Bourne, for he had established a thriving business at Denby near Derby at the beginning of the nineteenth century, when still in his twenties. Like the Doulton factory, Bourne produced containers for all manner of things, including gin, whisky, ink, blacking, meat and fish pastes – even hot water bottles. The hard, dense stoneware pottery made by Doulton, Bourne and their contemporaries would have consisted of very siliceous clay or a mixture of clay with much flint or sand added. Ordinary earthenware vessels, on the other hand, would have been produced from coarse, porous clays which provided the body for the bulk of the cheaper flat and hollow ware items produced at this time. At the other end of the scale, of course, porcelain, the hardest and finest earthenware, consisted largely of kaolin, and ware of this nature required high temperature firing.

Burslem, the mother town of the Potteries, first witnessed Henry Doulton when he bought the now famous Nile Street Works in 1877. But it was the Lambeth factory, acquired over sixty years earlier by Henry's father, which we have to thank for the fine variety of stoneware now sought so eagerly by collectors all over the world. Very much in evidence and usually accounting for a high proportion of any 'dig', stoneware inks, vinegar bottles, blacking pots and ginger beers can be found in abundance in most Victorian dumps. Cream jugs, ointment pots, historical flasks and transfer-printed whiskies are, however, rare by comparison. A possible reason for this may have been that such containers proved re-usable over a long period of time and were only thrown out when broken. It says much for the strength of stoneware in the main, though, that so many containers have survived in perfect or near-perfect condition. As for scarcer items of stoneware, some collectors are prepared to pay a great deal for unusual early marked specimens by firms like Doulton and Bourne which were originally sold for a few pence. In addition to decanters and flagons made for sale to the general public at Vauxhall Walk, for example, large quantities of advertisement whisky jugs were produced for firms beginning to appreciate the rewards from publicity. Undertakings of this type for Scottish and Irish distillers aiming chiefly but not entirely at the export trade were not uncommon between 1880 and 1930, and have consequently become very popular with collectors in many countries throughout the world. Some of these nineteenth-century flagons were cream based and decorated in colours or with relief figuring, but the majority were plain brown stoneware with printed or embossed trade marks and lettering. Necks were sometimes glazed a darker brown or blue. Some very attractive examples are found with an overall deep mottled blue colouring, but these would appear to be few in number.

Around 1875 Eliza Simmance designed a flagon for 'Melrose Highland Whisky' and she and other Doulton artists were responsible, in collaboration with the distillers, for almost all the designs. The names of some twenty distillers have been noted for whom the Lambeth Pottery made flagons, and there may well have been more. Some, such as John Dewar & Sons, ordered flagons in different shapes, decorations and sizes at various times, and between 1883 and 1889 a special range was produced at Lambeth decorated with etchings of Scottish landscapes and castles. There is, therefore, considerable scope for collectors in this field.

A Doulton & Co catalogue for 1889 shows that, among other things,

Doulton spirits bottle   Doulton ale jug   Doulton tap-hole bottle
(Line drawings by Norman Stockton)

the firm manufactured ground- and screwed-stoppered bottles for acids and spirits, extract pots for soups and jellies, jam jars, mustard pots, bung jars, household jars in enamelled stoneware, tamarind pans (the fruit of this large tropical tree was used by the Victorians in medicine and as relish), pipkins, and numerous bottles for ale, ginger beer, porter, ink, polish, quicksilver, furniture cream, disinfecting powder, scent and blacking.

It is perhaps interesting to note here that Charles Dickens spent some five months at the age of twelve labelling pots of blacking in a factory at Hungerford Stairs on the Thames just below the Strand. This would have been in 1824, and due to its close proximity to Lambeth, which was about a mile down river, it was well within the bounds of possibility that young Dickens handled a good many of the Doulton blacking pots. In fact an account book for this period reveals that the Lambeth factory's main output was of bottles for beer, spruce beer (then popular as a preventive against scurvy, a disease resulting from a deficiency of vitamin C and common among sailors who lived for long periods without fresh vegetables), oil bottles, paste jars, gallipots (ointment pots) and indeed blacking pots. Some of the trade sale prices at this time included 2s (10p) per dozen for half-pint bottles such as ales and ginger beers, anchovy jars, etc, and 12s 6d (62½p) per gross for druggists phials. A thrower on piece rate (work paid for by the piece) would earn 1s 3d (6p approx) for each hundred half-pint bottles made and 2s per hundred for anchovy jars.

The potter threw the clay on a horizontal wheel which, until the

Blacking bottles, tallest 14½cm (*Author's collection*)

Assorted glass and earthenware bottles. Milk glass bottle (*third from left*), 11½cm
(*Author's collection*)

1890s was hand-operated by a small boy or girl. The later 'kick wheel' had the advantage of being self-operated by the thrower, leaving his hands free to work the clay on the revolving platform. Power-driven wheels using water and (towards the turn of the century) electricity, were also made use of in the pottery industry. Raw clay was fashioned on the thrower's wheel with an accuracy akin to mechanisation, each lump of clay being directed by the craftsman's fingers into a precision-made article.

By the 1890s, and probably due to improved methods of production or to increasing competition from glass, or both, prices for stoneware bottles had been almost halved. Half-pint ales and ginger beers, for example, were being sold to the trade at around 12s 6d per gross. Half-pint anatto bottles (anatto being an orange-red dye from Central America used increasingly by the Victorians to colour cheese) sold at 14s (70p) per gross, and tiny half-ounce 'bellied' and 'upright' scent bottles at 12s (60p) per twelve dozen.

When Joseph Bourne of Denby was granted a patent for making non-vitreous stoneware bottles, these were, as already mentioned, made on a thrower's wheel by hand. The bottles were then fired in rectangular kilns and common salt thrown on to the kiln fires. The salt vapour subsequently combined with the clay to produce the shiny, brown surface coating – hence the term 'salt glaze'. But as well as making plain bottles and containers for all kinds of liquid, Bourne's craftsmen produced excellent examples of the detailed care always given to design and production by the family. Among such items were spirit flasks which, although appearing to be ornaments, were in fact cleverly designed to hold liquor – usually 'mother's ruin' or gin. Dealt with in more detail later in the book, these 'reform flasks' are rarely found in Victorian rubbish dumps, being almost certainly handed down from generation to generation. Fine collector's pieces, these flasks were fashioned in the effigies of famous people who supported the first major Reform Bill in the 1830s. Doulton & Co are also known to have made similar flasks, although perhaps not so politically evocative – merman and mermaid figures being among the better known.

Entrepreneurs of high standing, the Bournes had potbanks producing stoneware containers at Belper, Ilkeston, Denby, Codnor Park and Shipley at various times throughout Victoria's reign. William, the eldest son, was in fact a partner in the Nile Street (Burslem) pottery of Pinder, Bourne & Co which was eventually sold to Doulton's of Lambeth and is still the site of their present china factory. An observer in 1828 noted that the Bourne Codnor Park Works was:

visual stimulation. Stoneware bottles and flagons were ideal and such containers were used well into the twentieth century in England by the vinegar and cider makers who would supply large capacity vessels to retailers who then filled their customers' own bottles. Porter and stout underwent the same procedure in Ireland and England respectively. Attempts were made by the pottery manufacturers to stem the flow away from stoneware containers through the introduction of bottles with coloured shoulders (red, green, blue, etc) but the consensus of opinion was, for bottles for the home market at any rate, in favour of glass.

By the time the nineteen-year-old Victoria was crowned in 1838, the glass container was being used for an increasing range of commodities. As demand grew, new methods to increase production were sought. The actual constituents of glass, however, remained virtually the same as those used by the Egyptians, Syrians, Greeks and Romans, except for the use of a natural carbonate of soda known as natron. Employed by the early glassmakers as a flux together with silica in the form of sand, natron was eventually superseded by soda ash obtained from various species of seaweed. Barilla, an impure alkali extracted from kelp, was imported from Sicily and Spain, the ashes of the weed having been calcinated for carbonate of soda. Various plants in England containing large quantities of alkali were formerly burnt to provide potash for glassmaking, being known collectively as glasswort. Bracken or fern was one such plant used frequently in the Middle Ages by those glass-makers working far inland and for whom supplies of seaweed were restricted. Manufacturing chemists, however, were supplying potash to most of the leading glass manufacturers in Britain by the middle of the nineteenth century, the substance eventually being produced from salt and carbon dioxide. Sand, of course, was plentiful, being dug from river beds and shorelines with relative ease.

Because sand invariably contained particles of iron in some measure, only coloured glass (mainly in dark greens and browns) was produced in Victorian times up until 1845 and the abolition of glass duties. Previously, a relatively small duty of 8s 9d (44p) per hundredweight was levied on bottle-glass as opposed to eleven times that amount on flint-glass. This differential duty prevented the manufacture of the 'common' bottle and the 'flint' bottle (a clear glass container then used by the pharmaceutical trade) in the same glassworks, and was due to a limitation imposed by law on the use of certain materials in bottle-glass. Once restrictions were lifted, however, bottle-makers began adding manganese, a black mineral used as an oxidising agent, to their 'common' bottle mix. This produced a colourless metal and therefore a transparent container, which was quickly exploited by the newly emergent 'soft drinks' industry.

To make glass, a mixture of silica and potash had to be fired to a temperature of 1300° C, the metal at this point becoming adhesive and pliable. Additives such as limestone, red lead and chalk were used to produce strength and sparkle in hollow containers, while small amounts of metallic oxides such as copper, iron and cobalt brought forth a rich variety of colours and shades in greens, browns and blues. For glass-makers producing window glass and such items requiring as clear a finish as possible, decolourised glass was made with a manganese, selenium or arsenic additive. With commodities sold in bottles, it soon became obvious that shaded glass (like stoneware) prevented consumers from seeing unsightly particles that were inevitable with certain popular soft drinks. Increased amounts of iron oxide were therefore added to the melts to produce the dark greens, browns and blacks for these products. The latter 'black' glass, of course, could really be seen to be a very dark shade of green if held up to the light.

Tin or zinc oxide was used to produce 'milk' glass which became very popular in Germany and England in the field of cosmetics in the late nineteenth century. But probably the most easily adaptable metallic element available to the glassmaker was copper oxide. It was found that by regulating the furnace temperature whilst at the same time varying the quantity of the oxide to the mix a beautiful range of emerald greens, blues and light reds through pinks could be obtained. The most expensive Victorian glass to make was probably that which was dark red in colour. This again could be achieved at a controlled temperature by adding the correct amount of selenium. Prior to this discovery, dark red glass could only be made by adding one ounce of gold to every sixty pounds of glass melt.

Glass was melted in pots (approximately 150cm high by 120cm wide) made of fireclay, some ten or so of these being employed in each furnace. Small pieces of glass from the manufactory and refuse glass (cullet) suitable for re-melting, were added to the raw materials and left to heat until the pots were ready to be 'worked'. Round beehive-shaped furnaces built of bricks and heated from the centre by means of flues accommodated the containers of molten glass around their perimeters, the glassmaker drawing his 'gather' or paraison of syrupy liquid by means of a hollow iron rod known as a blowing iron. This instrument was usually in the region of one hundred and fifty centimetres in length and thus allowed the artisan to obtain his gather in spite of the intense heat from the furnace. Having a consistency similar to syrup, the molten glass adhered easily to the metal end of the blowing rod and

Within a short time of his joining them, the Libbey organisation decided to form the Toledo Glass Company in order to expand some of the advanced ideas of its 'glass boffins'. This was in 1894. Soon Owens had built, with the aid of machinist William Bock, a hand machine for blowing bottles which had cost approximately fifty dollars to construct. Its first product was a four-ounce vaseline jar. Further development saw the machine make an eight-ounce soda water bottle and two years later Bock had built a six-arm revolving machine, the arms each having gathering and finishing moulds, capable of producing pint beer bottles. The machine was soon making between six and nine bottles a minute; thus assured of success, Edward Drummond Libbey formed the huge Owens Bottle Machine Company which from 1903 exploited the inventive genius of Michael Owens and his automatic bottle-blowing machine. It was not long before the firm went into production of other types of machine-made bottles including containers for milk, catsup (a variety of ketchup), fruit preserves and many more. Early in the twentieth century the company opened a plant at Manchester, England, for making beer bottles and one on the Rhine making mineral water containers at the rate of 35 million a year. Indeed the 100,000 pound giant 'suctional' brain child of this dynamic Virginian with its 10,000 component parts was described as follows by a German writer at the time of Owens' death in 1923:

It feeds itself with a fiery fluid of molten glass; sucks it up methodically, clutches it with iron hands, blows its breath into it, releases its grasp, nonchalantly drops a finished bottle – and moves on to take another fiery gulp. At the rate of 150 bottles a minute – for it has fifteen mouths and arms and pairs of hands – it goes on.

The age of automation within the glass industry was, without doubt, here to stay.

3
HOUSEHOLD CONTAINERS

In examining general or everyday containers used in the Victorian household, it might be useful to consider the buying power of the town dweller, especially from 1875 onwards. By this time the transition from an agrarian economy to a predominantly industrial one was virtually complete. Now much of the food which was once prepared in the home could no longer be provided in the back-to-back factory housing which lacked the facilities for producing eggs, milk, butter, cheese, vegetables, beer and the wealth of produce afforded to a cottage industry or mainly farming community.

Towns provided no such amenities and thus a market for commercially processed food was not only stimulated but also conducted on a large scale in Victorian cities and large towns. As population movement into industrial regions grew, so did the number of people in regular employment. They must also have felt the benefit from higher incomes, for it would appear that average working-class purchasing power was indeed higher in the towns than in the countryside.

As the retailing revolution became established, so too did the producers of glass bottles. From the 1860s onwards glass containers were increasingly used in the packaging of foodstuffs for retailing outlets. A high percentage of these bottles and jars would have been unembossed and aqua or bluish-green in colour, for it was only at the very end of the nineteenth century that vessels made from clearer glass were demanded by food manufacturers.

A good proportion of the makers of marmalades and jams, however, still clung steadfastly to earthenware pots when it came to marketing their products and some firms still use them to a lesser extent today. One notable Scottish manufacturer, James Keiller, whose Dundee factory was established as early as 1797, sold his 'Special Standard' marmalade throughout the world in white stoneware jars. Transfer-printed, with a motif of leaves surrounding the firm's name, many of these containers were made by the Newcastle manufactory of C. T.

Keiller marmalade jar (*Courtesy James Keiller & Son Limited*)

Maling who specialised in this type of product in the late 1880s.

The earliest known reference to the word 'marmalade' occurred in the reign of Henry VIII when it was used instead of the term 'jam'. The root word of marmalade is the Greek 'melimelon', meaning honey-apple, and describing an apple grafted on to a quince. From this developed the Portuguese and Spanish 'marmelada'. The bitter orange, used for making perfumed ointments and pomades, was introduced into Europe by the Moors in the eighth century AD. The tree quickly established itself in Andalucia, the southern province of Spain, and became abundant in and around the city of Seville. These bitter oranges were being used to make a preserve similar to what we now know as marmalade as early as the 1490s, but it was the wife of grocer John Keiller who is thought to have created orange marmalade by boiling Seville oranges with sugar in the same manner as she had made quince jelly. It was their son, James, who decided to put his mother's invention to the commercial test and the first Keiller factory was established in Dundee's Albert Square at the end of the eighteenth century.

Another well-known Scottish preserves manufacturer was James Robertson. He began as a young grocer in the village of Paisley in the late 1850s when, together with his wife Marion, he sought a proprietary name to protect their fast-selling brand of home-made marmalade. This simple recipe of pure fruit juice, sugar and fine shreds of orange peel, plus a special method of cooking, was thus given the name 'Golden Shred'. In order to produce Marion Robertson's unique clear marmalade with its golden shreds, each orange was separated into its components and put painstakingly back together again. The fullest use was made of every part of the orange – even the pips – to ensure the highest possible quality for the finished product. The Robertsons' marmalade was originally packed in stone jars with parchment lids, but later the jars were wrapped around with paper and the labels stuck to the outside of this.

In late Victorian times, no less than one third of the total female population in Britain between the ages of fifteen and twenty were domestic servants. It is hardly surprising then that the larger households would set aside perhaps one or two weeks each year for the making of preserves, including marmalade, the kitchen staff often producing enough to last for twelve months.

One of the first marmalades that could be bought over the counter in England was produced by the wife of an Oxford grocer, Frank Cooper, in the 1870s and soon became a recognised status symbol with the dons and undergraduates at the university. The staff at the firm's Victoria Buildings manufactory prepared jams, jellies, bottled fruits and marmalades with great care, the latter being packed in large, brown earthenware jars tied down with paper labels and covers. Oxford dons, like the majority of middle and upper class Victorians, ate well at breakfast for a leisurely start to the day was then considered one of the advantages of affluence. Breakfast in the declining years of the Victorian age would have included such delights as devilled kidneys, grilled kippers, kedgeree (a dish of fish, rice and eggs), coddled eggs, fried eggs, scrambled eggs, liver sausage and, if you had a hangover from the meal of the previous evening, raw eggs. This weighty Victorian menu was not one to be selected from: members of the family and guests were expected to sample a portion of each. The final course would have been plenty of toast, marmalade, and tea or coffee.

Oddly enough, tea was not in use in England until the late 1650s and although it became a fashionable drink it remained expensive because of having to be imported from China in fast tea-clippers. With the establishment of plantations in Assam and Ceylon in the 1830s, however, tea became more competitive in price and was never really

Assorted Victorian preserves jars, tallest 15½cm (*Author's collection*)

ousted by coffee. On the other hand, coffee had been drunk in Arabia from the fourteenth century, but did not become popular in Europe until some 300 years later when coffee-houses were opened in London. The Victorians were great experimenters with herbs and wild plants of all kinds and it was established that chicory, a plant belonging to the Compositae and growing wild in Britain, when mixed with coffee gave it a distinct bitter flavour and rich colouring. By the beginning of the 1870s coffee was being imported on a larger scale than tea, selling at 1s 6d (7½p) per pound as opposed to cheap varieties of its rival at 2s 3d (11p) per pound.

Extracts or essences of coffee were on sale at most grocers and chemists by the 1880s and indeed the Edinburgh manufacturing chemists, Thomas Symington and Company, were offering a whole range of coffee blends. Their 'Essence of Dandelion' coffee, for example, combined the 'well-known medicinal qualities of the dandelion (*Taraxacum*) with the refreshing and dietetic properties of coffee.' An advertisement from the Edinburgh and Leith Post Office Directory (1880–1) illustrates the range of essences manufactured by the firm at that time, including their latest preparation, 'Edinburgh Coffee and Milk'. This was composed of pure condensed milk combined with the finest extract of coffee and a suitable portion of chicory. The range was marketed in two-piece moulded aqua glass bottles with the contents

41

and firm's name embossed in perpendicular lettering. The company, now trading under the name of Scott & Orr, still exists, but as chemists and druggists they now manufacture mainly health food beverages.

Rather more slender and attractive glassware bottles in olive green were used by the firm of W. P. Branson to sell their coffee extract, whilst the Nottingham firm of Newball & Mason availed themselves of containers in light blue glass to market their essence of coffee and chicory. But probably one of the better-known Victorian firms still trading in this field today is that of R. Paterson & Sons Ltd of Glasgow, makers of the famous 'Camp Coffee'. They began business in 1845 when they bottled pickles, and have been producing 'Camp' since 1883. The present bottle label is a modification of the celebrated original design based on a portrait of the Scottish general, Sir Hector Macdonald, who fought in the Boer War. Innovations to this label of renown were made as early as 1902, but an advertisement taken from an old pamphlet of the time clearly shows that the bottle had a cork stopper and was embossed with the firm's name and the words 'Camp Coffee & Chicory'. The firm stopped embossing bottles in 1926 because they were being re-used for disinfectants.

The 1870s, of course, saw the introduction of carbolic acid by Joseph Lister and the consequent development of many different types of disinfectant. Advantages far outweighed the dangers, and Victorians were quick to take account of the hygienic benefits stemming from a whole new range of products. By 1888, for example, the Sanitas Co Ltd of Bethnal Green, London, were offering in their November price list bottles of disinfecting fluid, disinfecting oil, disinfecting emulsion, insecticide, liquid soap, toilet fluid, pots of disinfecting jelly and large wickered jars for bulk supply. The company even sold bottles of animal soap at 1s each and disinfecting furniture cream at 8s (40p) per dozen bottles. A considerable number of these late Victorian disinfectant containers have been found in dumps throughout Britain, probably the most common being those which once contained 'Sanitas' disinfecting fluid. Their contents were claimed to be 'absolutely non-poisonous', and were said to 'purify and revivify the air'. The bottles were used in conjunction with a specially made spray similar to those attached to Edwardian and other early twentieth-century scent containers.

The Yorkshire disinfectant company Izal, which was established as the chemical subsidiary of Newton, Chambers & Co of Thorncliffe in 1883, appointed their first consulting chemist in that year and soon began to experiment with carbolic acid and carbolic disinfecting powders. The first brief experiments with the making of 'Izal' occurred

(*Left*) Dripping jar 10cm; (*right*) 'Virol' jar – marrow-bone preparation for children and invalids 8½cm (*Author's collection*)

in 1886 and by the turn of the century it was being supplied to the Admiralty, the Army, the Board of Works and the Birmingham Corporation and had been registered as a trade mark all over the world. The power of advertising was accepted as being of great importance to the advancement of the company's products, and it was agreed to spend £5,500 on the advertising of Izal alone between May and September of 1893. Indeed at the company's annual meeting on 19 April 1894, it was disclosed that over £8,000 had been spent on successful publicity based on a scheme submitted by advertising agents T. B. Browne Ltd the previous year.

It might be pointed out here to new collectors that there are a number of quite attractively tapered screw-topped Izal bottles in dark green glass on the market. These partially ribbed containers have a single letter on each shoulder making up the brand name and bear the date 1893 on their base. The date, of course, refers to the registration of contents and trade mark and not to the year in which the container was produced. Closer inspection will reveal mould seams passing right through the neck and external threading, indicative of early twentieth-century production methods.

Before 1870, advertising space on hoardings, vehicles and in newspapers was taken only by those with something unusual to sell, such as patent medicines. By 1875, however, advertisers were beginning

43

to stress special services to customers, including reduced prices. For the entrepreneur, making certain that as many people as possible knew about his products soon became part of his firm's life-blood and his own survival, so that when trade was seen to outstrip over-the-counter sales it simply stimulated the incentive for increased advertising.

American dairies were probably the first to take advantage of bottles and jars as vehicles for advertising slogans regarding milk and cream. But it was well into the twentieth century before legislation in Britain and America made it an offence to sell milk to the public other than in a sealed bottle. In-bottle sterilisation of milk based on Pasteur's successful experiments was being practised in Denmark and Germany as early as 1880, whilst in New York private families could have milk delivered in sealed vessels of porcelain or glass and with special fastenings, capable of holding from one pint to two quarts. It is known that milk was supplied to Queen Victoria in containers with porcelain caps which bore the reference 'By Appointment', this undoubtedly referring to George Barham's Express Dairy Co Ltd. In the 1860s, Barham had been the first to use railways for transporting bulk milk from the country. When an outbreak of rinderpest (a malignant and contagious cattle disease) caused the Government to order the destruction of all London cattle in 1865, Barham was the only one capable of preventing a milk famine in the capital.

As with London, New York drew its milk supplies in the final quarter of the nineteenth century from dairies 100 to 200 miles away. A container known as the 'Lester' can became popular during this period, being made of strong glass and having a glass lid which was fastened by a metallic clamp. Possibly the earliest known American milk bottle is the 'Thatcher', named after its inventor, a New York druggist. A number of reproductions in a variety of colours are known to be on sale, but originals are of clear glass and have glass tops held in position by metallic swing stoppers. A similar hermetically-sealed milk container was the 'Crystal' jar which had a glass top screwed down upon a rubber ring. The vessel's neck was wide enough to permit the removal of cream if required, and a small ladle could be purchased for this purpose. Incidentally, the British Food and Drugs Act of 1899 empowered a standard to be fixed below which the fats and solids content of cows' milk should not fall; the same *quantum* applied in the United States.

Bottles containing filtered, medicated and other milks were on display at Manchester's Jubilee Exhibition of 1887, and within seven years their exhibitor, Anthony Hailwood, a north-of-England dairy-

Evolution of the milk bottle (*Line drawing by Norman Stockton*)

man, had developed a method of sterilising milk, the liquid being sold to the public in swing-stoppered bottles. Indeed it is thought that sterilised milk was introduced generally in England about the middle of the 1890s for a London firm, Mortlock Sterilised Milk Co Ltd, stated at this time that they were unable to keep pace with the demand for their product and that other dairies were beginning to introduce it into various parts of the country.

It would appear that towards the end of Victoria's reign, Britain was actually importing milk bottles from Europe. Possibly mould-blown with sheared lips, their necks were welded afterwards, but variety in shape and capacity made filling and closure by machine difficult. The improvement of dairy machines called for better glass containers, the demand being met initially by suppliers in the United States and Canada using the latest and very accurate Owens automatic bottle-making machines. Soon the machines themselves were being imported and bottle-making in Britain entered upon a whole new era. Design became of great importance, for not only had the law governing weights and measures to be complied with, but it was soon realised that the clarity and shape of the bottle played an important part in attracting the consumer, particularly with regard to the visible depth of cream.

The milk of goats and cows was fed to early Victorian infants in boat-shaped feeders made of porcelain which had cork-stoppered apertures to receive the liquid and elongated teat-shaped necks. Many had coloured or transparent glazes, but later versions were decorated with underglaze patterns. The majority of baby-feeders found in British dumps, however, are in clear or aqua glass and belong to one of three basic designs: the rarer 'Hamilton', the 'pancake' and the 'stand-up'. A variety of stoppers including cork, porcelain, wood, pewter and glass appeared on these bottles, the rubber tube and teat becoming popular with Victorians who wished to avoid nursing their babies during feeding.

The Piccadilly firm of R. J. Reuter claimed that their 'Aseptus' feeding bottle, which retailed at 1s (5p), was made of English glass, had a seamless and self-cleansing teat of best English make, incorporated a regulating screw and could be kept quite clean and free from germs – hence its name. Another London firm of druggists, H. Gilbertson & Sons, advertising their 'Graduated' flattened-oval feeding bottles at 6d (2½p) each in 1890 claimed:

These bottles are graduated to Tablespoons and Ounces, which enables the milk to be reduced to a uniform strength, and acts as a guide to mothers and nurses in giving food in regular quantities; also, when adding Lime Water or other simple remedies, no spoon or measure is necessary.

William Mather's 'Improved' infant's feeding bottles of the stand-up variety were available in the 1870s, and had ceramic screw tops and internal glass tubes. An enterprising man by any standards, Mather began business as a medical plaster-maker in London's Fleet Street in the late 1850s, manufacturing adhesive applications of curative substances (ointments, etc) on linen or muslin dressings. As a wholesale and druggist's sundryman, he dealt in surgical instruments and medical glass, and Victorian directories of the 1870s listed him as 'Court Plaister' and proprietor of Mather's Royal Balsamic Plasters. A great believer in diversification, Mather's factory at Hulme in Cheshire was even producing chemical fly paper and marking ink in addition to the many commodities it made for its Manchester and London outlets by the turn of the century. The feeding bottle wholesaling and retailing firm of S. Maw, Son & Sons was a name possibly as well known to Victorians for its variety of merchandise as to twentieth-century Elizabethans. Examples of pot lids manufactured for the London company and quite an assortment of Maw's feeders have found their way into many collections in recent years, and are extremely popular collectors' items when intact.

been employed by some confectioners for 'painting' their icing.

The age-old practice of 'washing' or watering down milk gave the liquid a bluish tint, especially with the cream removed as well. This was overcome to a certain extent by adding powdered chalk, but for those members of the public who preferred a seemingly rich and creamy-yellow yield, the dairyman was obliged to introduce the additive, anatto. This harmless vegetable substance was also used in butter and cheese for the same purpose, and thousands of stoneware anatto bottles were made in the second half of the nineteenth century. Light-brown glassware bottles bearing the words 'butter color' and purporting to come from the United States have also been found in late-Victorian dumps, Tomlinson & Co's 'Butter Color' being one of them. These containers of almost yellow glass would certainly have made their contents appear (to use a current advertising phrase) 'sun-kissed'. Like anatto, another additive which was not detrimental was arrowroot. A nutritious starch could be prepared from this tropical plant, and this was sometimes mixed in with cream by the dairyman to thicken it. A rather more lethal ploy, however, was the inclusion of red lead as a colouring matter for certain cheeses.

Some of the more spurious brewers around mid-century were making beers with an infusion of copperas or green vitriol. The iron content of this ferrous sulphate probably did give a brew added strength as well as producing a fine head, but sulphuric acid under any name is not really beneficial to the lining of the stomach. The highly poisonous alkaloid, strychnine, used in medicine as a stimulant, was reputed to give beer its bitter taste. Many breweries throughout the country were thought to be using this illegal method, and some were duly exposed by the Analytical and Sanitary Commission during the 1840s and 1850s. The great Burton-on-Trent brewing establishment of Allsopp & Sons, when accused of such malpractice, immediately invited random sampling by the Commission. Somewhere in the region of four dozen samples were taken from various Allsopp brews on the insistence of Henry Allsopp himself and found to contain nothing else but malt, hops and the famous Burton waters. But unfortunately all breweries were not as scrupulous as the Midlands company, and many drinkers suffered gastro-enteritis and even convulsions which caused paralysis after consuming adulterated beer.

In the better-off households, both cook and butler would be expected to procure food and wines of the best quality. Wine was one of the butler's responsibilities, but although it was his duty to decant it for daily use and to record the amount consumed, the cellar keys were always in the possession of the master. This situation would hardly have applied to a first-class cook, however, who would not allow interference with the way in which she ran her kitchen. The lady of the house often stood in awe of her, as did tradesmen who sought her custom. A good cook of the 1880s knew exactly what she wanted for her kitchen and could usually get it: a generous cut of meat for 6d (2½p) per pound; poultry at 1s 6d (7½p); fresh cream at 1s 6d per pint; new laid eggs at 2s (10p) per dozen; fresh butter for 9d (4p) per pound; pure cider (for the servants) at 1s (5p) per gallon, and so on. None of your left-overs here, and heaven help the butcher or poulterer who sold her bad meat or the dairyman reckless enough to deliver rancid butter or cheese.

The poor, however, suffered much at the expense of the well-to-do, having to take what was left at the end of the day – rotting meat, withering vegetables and stale bread. It must be remembered that these were the days when refrigeration was in its infancy and the preservation of foodstuffs by chilling or freezing had a long way to go to achieve perfection. Aware of the need for some form of preservative for perishable goods, a number of compounds claiming practicability emerged on the market. One such commodity was 'Preservine', an antiseptic salt manufactured by the Bedford firm of S. Mann & Co. Salt or chloride of sodium had been used for many years for seasoning and preserving food, but Mann's product was claimed 'free from colour, taste or smell, and as wholesome as the bread we eat.' The final phrase was hardly dependable advertising, because at that particular time bread contained a number of unwholesome additives in the form of chalk and alabaster. The advert went on:

> ... Milk is guaranteed to keep perfectly sweet for eight days during the most sultry weather, and butter for any length of time. On any food likely to turn sour its preserving qualities are marvellous. No more tainted meat, sausages, fish, poultry, &c. by using PRESERVINE.

Another seemingly well known product for preserving foodstuffs in the 1880s was 'Glacialine', which claimed not only to preserve perishables but also to 'defy time'. The sole manufacturers and patentees of this commodity, the Antitropic Company of Glasgow, issued containers with labels lithographed in five colours and bearing their 'globe' trade mark. According to its makers, Glacialine was quite capable of keeping milk, butter and eggs fresh in the hottest weather, and of preserving meat, fish and poultry to perfection in any climate.

A serious challenge to the butter-making side of dairying was an edible fat coloured to resemble butter and introduced into Britain in the 1870s. It had been invented by Mege-Mouries, a Frenchman attempting to find a cheap substitute for butter. The product was called 'margarine', and although scorned by the wealthy, proved a welcome alternative with the working-class housewife due to its being half the price of its rival. Cheap imported meat and grain also improved the lot of the late-Victorian working man and his family, and in the towns potted, bottled and tinned commodities such as fruit, jams, pastes and pickled vegetables were beginning to fall within the scope of the ordinary family. Trades such as preserves manufacturing, grocery, greengrocery and pickling increased by 80 per cent in the 1880s, and by 1891 the food industry employed some 500,000 people.

The preservation of food (particularly fruit and vegetables) had been undertaken by eighteenth-century housewives with limited success, but it was Frenchman Nicholas Appert who first expounded the principle of preserving food through heat and the elimination of air. Strong glass bottles were filled, sealed and subjected to heat before being successfully tested with the French Navy during the Napoleonic Wars. Englishman Thomas Saddington's method was similar to that of Appert's except that he used wide-mouthed glass jars, filled them with meats, fish, cooked fruits or vegetables, and then put on loosely-fitting stoppers. The jars were then heated to a temperature of 170°F, their contents topped up with boiling water, and finally their stoppers tightened.

Satisfactory sealing of preserving jars remained a problem until 1858 when John Landis Mason, an American tin-smith from New Jersey, invented an air-tight zinc closure for use on screw-topped jars. Housewives were now able to preserve and store fruit and vegetables through the winter, and domestic food preservation became widespread in the United States. The one real disadvantage of the Mason closure was that the zinc inevitably came into direct contact with the contents of the jar, but Louis Boyd solved this problem in 1869 by fitting a porcelain lining inside the lid.

Because bottles and jars were still being made by hand in the nineteenth century, glass could only be used beneficially for foodstuffs that did not require a fully air-tight seal. Experiments with metal containers had been undertaken by Brian Donkin even before the young Victoria became queen, however, and by the time of her death in 1901 were beginning to gain a substantial footing as competitively priced packagings for all manner of goods. They were under consideration, for example, by Henry John Heinz for his '57 Varieties', a slogan which he invented in 1896. Up until then, Heinz had employed glass bottles for his products to show that no substitute ingredients were being used, a method successfully designed to win the confidence of the consumer in relation to factory-preserved foods.

The last two decades of the nineteenth century were years of great opportunity for the wholesaling, retailing and manufacturing entrepreneurs, and business boomed. Chain stores such as Lipton's, Maypole, Home & Colonial, Marks & Spencer and Sainsbury flourished, as did the select departmental stores like Harrod's and Fortnum & Mason's. Exciting foods, wines and relishes began to be imported from Europe and the British Empire, the public at last beginning to reap the benefits of refrigeration and forty years work in bacteriology.

For those affluent Victorians who knew that life could be sustained by bread and water, but also that it could be delightfully improved by caviar and champagne, the London firm of Fortnum & Mason proved the place to purchase the world's most fabulous foods. From the early 1700s the Fortnum half of the firm had had close connections with the Palace of St James, through the Royal Household of Queen Anne and later through that of Queen Charlotte. These links were undoubtedly responsible for the way in which the business developed, but there were also Fortnums with the same impeccable tastes in the East India Company. This English commercial company had been given the monopoly of trade between England and the East, and up until 1858 had supplied this country (and Fortnum & Mason's) with all manner of exotic spices, foods, relishes and beverages.

Delicacies such as boned portions of poultry and game in aspic jelly, decorated with lobsters and prawns; potted meats including ham, chicken and beef; anchovy paste and caviar; brandy-soaked cake with whipped cream; savoury patties and a range of fresh and dried fruits – all had been readily available at Fortnum & Mason's since the 1780s. But the Victorian era with its prosperity and its famous clubs like the Carlton, Crockford's, the Garrick and the Guards' demanded even more, and the firm opened a special department to provide concentrated luncheons which included tinned Scotch salmon and rich beef stews. By the mid-nineteenth century the better-off Victorians could procure Fortnum & Mason ready-roasted duck and green peas at 5s (25p); partridges, 2s 6d (12½p); real West Indian turtle, 10s (50p) per pound; and a whole truffled pheasant for 15s (75p).

The firm supplied ham, butter, cheese, honey, spices and cereals to Wellington's officers; sweetened cocoa powder for Parry's North West Passage Expedition of 1819; concentrated beef tea for Florence Nightingale in the Crimea; a lobster-salad and champagne hamper for Charles Dickens on Derby Day ('If I were on the turf, and had a horse to enter for the Derby, I would call that horse Fortnum & Mason, convinced that with that name he could beat the field.'); and advice to Prime Minister Gladstone on the problem of sugar duties.

As was the custom in the 1880s, certain members of the staff lived on the premises, for work began at a quarter to eight and early preparations had to be made. The firm's shop assistants would call at many stately residences in Mayfair, Belgravia, Bayswater and Kensington. Sometimes they would return from Buckingham Palace with some surprisingly modest orders from Queen Victoria – 'Two pots of Marmalade, 1s 8d' or 'Four Bottles of Oil, at 2s 6d'. The Prince of Wales, however, being a regular patron of the firm and a great connoisseur of table delicacies, often ordered such delights as Apricot Pulp, and Parmesan and Gruyère cheeses. Throughout the day the shop would be visited by the aristocracy and foreign dignitaries who would purchase, among other things, caviar, pâté de foie gras, Perigord pies (from the ancient French province) containing meat flavoured with truffles, guava jelly (made from the acid fruit of a tropical American tree), Spanish hams, boar's head, mangoes, and Carlsbad plums from Czechoslovakia.

Due the their capacity for obtaining rarities from virtually anywhere in the world, prestige establishments like Fortnum & Mason's and Harrod's were in a position to introduce a whole new concept of living to those rich enough to afford it. But as the Empire grew and more and more ordinary men and women were drafted abroad, demands for spices and relishes sampled in India, Africa and the Far East were often forthcoming on their return. Possibly one of the most insatiable demands from returning troops and servants of the crown was that for relishes. They quickly became popular with the Victorian masses, for they provided an exotic, piquant and welcome addition to the rather unexciting meals of the gastronomically uninitiated members of the public.

The recipe for Lea & Perrins 'Worcestershire Sauce', for example, was acquired from the old province of Bengal in the north-east of the Indian peninsula. John Lea and William Perrins, although sophisticated pharmacists and analytical chemists qualified to tackle a sauce recipe rich in Oriental exoticism and complicated in rare constituent, were disappointed with the initial result. The first few gallons made to assess the sauce's viability as a commercial proposition proved unpalatable and were consigned to the cellars in stone jars. The contents of these dust-covered and forgotten jars were later tasted again prior to throwing them away. The taste of the matured sauce was superlative. 'Worcestershire Sauce' was first produced commercially by Lea & Perrins in the city of Worcester in 1837, the year of the young Victoria's accession to the throne. The sauce was first served to the public in a Worcester chop-house (a fashionable type of Victorian

Cases of Lea & Perrins Sauce being loaded on to an LMS Railway horse-drawn dray, c 1840 (*Courtesy Lea & Perrins Limited*)

restaurant specialising in mutton and pork chops) during the 1830s and proved immediately successful.

The glass sauce container, with its elongated neck, was specially commissioned for Lea & Perrins in the late 1830s, and was originally fitted with a solid cork. Around 1850 it appears that the firm started to use bottles with a ledge finish to accommodate a cork ring and glass stopper, this method of closure being retained for over 100 years. The

Worcestershire Sauce bottles (*Courtesy Lea & Perrins Limited*)

First introduction of Lea & Perrins Worcestershire Sauce in a Worcester chop-house, c 1839 (*Courtesy Lea & Perrins Limited*)

Goodall, Backhouse & Co, Courtenay's and Massey's sauce bottles, tallest 22¼cm
including stopper (*Author's collection*)

reason for the long neck, and indeed for the filling of the bottle to the
base of the neck, was to allow space for the sauce to be shaken so that the
sediment which formed could be easily re-blended with the relish's
lighter ingredients.

The firm used bottles which were embossed with the words 'Lea &
Perrins' vertically, and 'Worcestershire Sauce' round the shoulder,
from about 1840 to 1890. These were mould-blown containers formed
in simple two-piece moulds with the neck finished separately in a small
press. The neck of the bottle and the neck finish were heated and then
fused together with a twisting motion which resulted in a slightly
spiralled mark in the neck itself. The very early containers bore a
distinctly greenish tinge, with the glass becoming clearer and the
bottles more accurate and refined as time went on. The mark 'A. C. B.
Company', often with a serial number, was at one time embossed on
the base of the bottles. The embossment, of course, referred to the bottle
manufacturer which is thought to be the Aire & Calder Bottle Company
of Castleford, although the firm of A. C. Bagley & Co also produced
bottles for Lea & Perrins at one time.

Due to its instant success and consequent long-term popularity, other manufacturers sought to imitate 'Worcestershire Sauce' even to the extent of attempting to reproduce similar packaging. Labels for the bottles were originally black and white, but shortly afterwards were changed to orange. The inclusion of a signature showing as white on an orange ground soon followed, and an Order from the Court of Chancery dated 24 April 1906 eventually granted Lea & Perrins the legal right to describe their product as 'The Original and Genuine'.

These famous nineteenth-century sauce bottles are in no way limited to Victorian dumps throughout the British Isles, for they have found their way to some most unusual places. Specimens have come to light, ironically enough, in Calcutta, where the recipe probably came from in the first place; further north beyond the Himalayan Mountains, nearly 12,000 feet above sea level in the forbidden city of Lhasa; the gold-fields of New South Wales; by archaeologists excavating the buried city of Te Wairoa in New Zealand, which had been engulfed by a volcanic eruption in 1886. When Lea & Perrins 'Worcestershire Sauce' advertisement appeared in the January of 1870 stating that the product was 'sold wholesale and for export by the proprietors, Worcester; Crosse & Blackwell, London; and retail by druggists, grocers, and oilmen generally throughout the world', the last phrase was obviously no exaggeration.

The Crosse & Blackwell firm, incidentally, although they had been established in their own right for many years, subscribed to the Victorian policy of acting as agents for selected brands of merchandise from other reputable companies. Their retail shop traded from London's Soho Square, and the firm had proudly held the Royal Appointment of Victoria without break from 1837. It was made clear from the beginning that the then young partners, Crosse and Blackwell, were of the opinion that the only sure foundation on which to build a thriving organisation was quality. Consequently, they sought the advice of the world's greatest masters of cuisine, including Charles Francatelli, who later became chef to the Queen. The company's price list for 1860 included twenty-five varieties of soup, twenty selections of crystallised fruits, many liqueurs, and a vast choice of game pâtés, jams, honey and similar delicacies.

In the same year that Crosse & Blackwell acquired their Appointment to Queen Victoria, the sauce manufacturing firm of Goodall, Backhouse & Co became established in Leeds. The company had built up an enviable trade by the 1890s, but like so many firms with manufactures favoured by the public they were inevitably faced with the problem of imitators. Eventually they were forced to take a rival

Yorkshire firm of sauce makers, Holbrook & Co, to court over their trade mark 'Yorkshire Relish'. Apparently, Messrs Holbrook & Co had produced a sauce and called it 'Yorkshire Relish' in imitation of the product already on sale. Goodall, Backhouse & Co thus were left with no alternative but to commence action against Holbrook's. The case carried on for over two years, finally ending in the House of Lords where it was ruled that the words 'Yorkshire Relish' indicated only the product of Goodall, Backhouse & Co and nobody else. Bottles of both sauce companies turn up regularly in dumps of the late 1800s, as do sauce containers belonging to the Worcester firms of Mellor & Co and Courtenay & Co who operated from the city's Bridge Street and South Quay respectively. Harvey's sauce bottles are also fairly common to dump diggers, for this London firm from Portman Square was established long before Victoria came to the throne. A number of their large anchovy paste lids have become favourite collectors items because they have the royal crest of William IV included in their underglaze design. Harvey's sauce advertisements from the late Victorian era carried the following caution:

The admirers of this celebrated sauce are particularly requested to observe that each bottle, prepared by E. Lazenby and Son, bears the label used so many years, signed ELIZABETH LAZENBY.

But if leading shop suppliers like Lea & Perrins and Goodall, Backhouse & Co sometimes found the going hard, so too did the majority of Victorian shop assistants for different reasons. Most of them worked every day of the week except Sunday, and had to be at work by at least seven o'clock in the morning, and often much earlier. A half day might have been granted on Mondays if business was slow, but only from two o'clock in the afternoon. Most shops stayed open until nine o'clock in the evening during the week, and later on Saturdays. Indeed, assistants were lucky to finish work much before ten o'clock in the evening on weekdays and twelve o'clock midnight on Saturdays, this being due to the tidying up which had to be undertaken after closing. Hence the preference arose in many of the larger shops for employing unmarried men who could sleep on the premises. Fortunately, attempts were made to stop this exploitation of stores employees around the turn of the century, and finally in 1912 a law was passed restricting the shops opening times.

5
MEDICINES

In the generic sense the term 'medicine' covers every form of curative treatment for bodily and mental ailments and includes the study of the causes of disease. It would seem to have had its inauguration as a science in ancient Greece between 700 and 600 BC, although it was not until the nineteenth century that medicine was revolutionised in the western world.

Momentous strides in surgery were made possible by the safe and effective use of anaesthetics and also by the ability of surgeons to eradicate the harmful bacteria which caused infections through the increasing use of antiseptics. Prior to 1846, speed of operation was essential to the attributes of a successful surgeon, for the resultant pain produced shock which, if prolonged, could in itself be fatal.

Humphry Davy, the English chemist, discovered the effect of nitrous oxide as early as 1799 and indeed suggested its possible use in surgery, but it was not until 1842 that a surgical operation was performed under an inhaled anaesthetic. Ether, a light, volatile fluid produced by the distillation of alcohol with sulphuric acid had also been known for its desensitising qualities for some time when William Thomas Green Morton, an American dentist, first employed it successfully in 1846 and by November of that year it was being used in Britain. James Young Simpson, the Scottish obstetrician, originated the use of ether as an anaesthetic in childbirth in January 1847 and by the end of the year had discovered an even better desensitiser in chloroform. The advantages of chloroform were many, for it was not explosive and could be administered in much smaller doses than nitrous oxide or ether. Young continued to champion its use against hostile medical and religious pressure until its application at the birth of Victoria's youngest son, Leopold, in 1853, rendered it generally acceptable.

Prior to the 1860s the other major obstacle to surgery, that of infection, had still to be dealt with effectively. By 1863, however, both the American physician, Oliver Wendell Holmes, and the Hungarian obstetrician, Ignaz Phillip Semmelweiss, had discovered that puerperal fever was contagious. Indeed, it was Semmelweiss who realised the possibility of this disease being conveyed by uncleanliness. Appalled by the heavy death-rate in the Vienna maternity hospital where he worked, the obstetrician thus introduced antiseptics and the death-rate fell dramatically from 12 per cent to $1\frac{1}{4}$ per cent within months. Florence Nightingale, too, had realised that bad sanitary arrangements in hospitals caused frightful mortality when she set about nursing the wounded from Inkermann in November 1854. She was responsible for reducing the death-rate considerably as a direct result of her hygienically-trained nursing staff. But it was Louis Pasteur, a French chemist, who in 1865 finally proved that infection was in all cases due to germs, and it was on his findings that the modern study of bacteriology was based. A year later the English surgeon, Joseph Lister, introduced the antiseptic system (using carbolic acid) which was to revolutionise modern surgery. Working on wounds, septicaemia and splenic fever in the 1870s, the German bacteriologist, Robert Koch, went on to isolate the killer disease of the lungs called tuberculosis and later that of the cholera bacillus, although it was not until the 1920s that a vaccine was used to prevent the former and more recently injections of saline fluid were effectively adopted against the latter. The Victorian age also witnessed the discovery of X-rays by the German physicist Wilhelm Konrad Röntgen, which were later used to destroy cancer cells. The Polish born physicist, Marie Curie, was investigating the nature of uranium rays in the 1890s, and, just after the death of Queen Victoria, had succeeded in isolating the pure elements of polonium (named after Mme Curie's native Poland) and radium, which were both used for cancer therapy.

The problems of the mind were also first tackled on a scientific basis in the late nineteenth century when the Austrian psychiatrist, Sigmund Freud, came to believe that mental illness resulted from fears of the past and of the future. Rejecting Josef Breuer's cathartic method, which employed a hypnotic technique, Freud developed the method of free association which still remains the basic procedure in modern psychoanalysis. This, then, was the scientifically progressive medical backcloth against which the rather more colourful world of patent medicines existed and thrived in Victorian Britain.

Earthenware and glass containers had been used for the storage of medicines in one form or another for hundreds of years, and by the nineteenth century were being employed on a commercial basis. Indeed by the 1880s it was often the shape of the bottle rather than the contents that provoked a sale, and more and more containers of unusual outline began to invade the market. Robert Turlington's pear-shaped 'Balsam

'Daffy's Elixir' bottles with counterfeit container to the right, 13cm and 15cm respectively
(*Author's collection*)

of Life' was easily identified, as was the conical glass vial which contained the famous opium and treacle concoction known as 'Godfrey's Cordial', Dalby's 'Carminative', 'Daffy's Elixir', Fisher's 'Seaweed Extract', Price's 'Glycerine' and Dr Silby's 'Solar Tincture', too, were all cure-alls largely dependent upon the colour and unusual design of their containers.

That wealthy Victorians ate gluttonously is well known, so that it is not really surprising that a lucrative market for over-eating remedies existed. Leading newspapers and journals teemed with advertisements for patent medicines claiming instant relief for sufferers from indigestion, acidity, flatulence, bile, liver disorders and the like. The after-effects of gormandising could be so uncomfortable and distressing that the victim was ready to try almost anything to dispel the feeling that he was at death's door. Dicey & Co's 'True Daffy's Elixir' would appear to have been exactly what they needed:

This most excellent medicine has been faithfully prepared for nearly a century, from the purest drugs and spirits that can be procured, at the original warehouse, 10 Bow Churchyard, London, and has been attended with the fullest success in the cure of the Gravel, Stone, Spasms, Pains in the Breast, the most excruciating fits of Cholic, and in all complaints of the Stomach and Bowels.

This advert appeared on Saturday 17 August 1850, but an earlier breakdown of the mixture claimed that it consisted of a startling combination of:

aniseed – used as a carminative and flavouring
cochineal – a red dye made from insects
elecampane – a plant, the leaves and root of which were used as a tonic and stimulant
fennel – a plant from which the oil was extracted for use as a carminative
jalap – a Mexican climbing plant yielding a purgative drug
liquorice – used in pharmacy for masking bad taste in medicines
manna – juice obtained from the bark of ash and larch and used in medicine as a sweetener
parsley – the aromatic leaves of this herb were used for seasoning
raisins – frequently used in beer and wine making to retain body
rhubarb – roots used medicinally as a purgative
saffron – the juice from this plant was used for orange colouring and for flavouring
senna – a laxative from cassia bark

These ingredients, believe it or not, were then steeped in two gallons of brandy in specified quantities and allowed to mature prior to being bottled for sale to the general public. The medicine was dispensed in 2s (10p) and 2s 9d (13½p) glass containers bearing labels which warned against fraudulent imitations: 'See that "Dicey & Co" are engraved on the Government Stamp, all others being counterfeit and worthless preparations.' Indeed 'Daffy's Elixir' was one of the most widely counterfeited cure-alls of the nineteenth century, and the genuine eight-sided bottles embossed with the words 'Unless the name of Dicey & Co is in the stamp over the cork the medicine is counterfeit' are highly prized among collectors.

Working on the premise that people will often pay more for a commodity because they subconsciously want to convince themselves that they are getting better value with a more expensive item, Dr Solomon's 'Cordial Balm of Gilead' unashamedly sold at 10s 6d (52½p) a bottle to our Victorian ancestors – but then it did claim to relieve nervous disorders, hard drinking, excess of grief and dissipated pleasure. The true 'Balm of Gilead' was resin obtained from a plant of the Burseraceae family and used in the East as a perfume and for its healing properties. Making use of these facts, the vendors of Solomon's 'Cordial' stated that 'thousands in the West Indies have been restored from the yellow fever (an endemic infective fever of the tropics, now known to be carried by the mosquito) and the jaws of death by the Cordial Balm of Gilead.' By contrast Salisbury chemist, Edwin J. Orchard, supposedly cured hundreds with his safe and harmless 'Cure for Deafness'. Dellar's 'Essence for Deafness', an 1870s rival, cured not only deafness but 'noises in the ears' as well. Tender feet could be eased with Condy's 'Fluid'; chilblains, rheumatism and lumbago remedied with a 2s 9d (14p) bottle of Whitehead's 'Essence of Mustard'; neuralgia conquered ('Why suffer thus?') with 'St Jacob's Oil'; whilst the 'only certain cure for rheumatism' was 'Hampton Oils' with stated sales of some 60,000 bottles each year. Mander, Weaver & Co, the Wolverhampton suppliers of 'Hampton Oils', issued this quaintly worded testimony in June 1856:

> Sir,
> With respect to the Hampton Oils I cannot give them too good a name. They cured me of a lame leg of thirty years standing, although the doctors at the General Hospital, Birmingham, told me there was no cure for me. They have also cured me of a complaint in my teeth and gums. I am very happy to say I am now quite well.
> Your humble servant,
> Sarah Smith.

The business of Mander, Weaver & Co originated in 1773 and was a manufacturing as well as a dispensing concern. They were taken over in 1873 by Reade Brothers whose bottles and ointment pots such as 'Kowkow', 'Chest Balsam', 'The Egyptian Ointment', 'Cattle Drench', and others, continually crop up in dumps dating from 1880 to 1900.

Poisons were readily sold over the counter to anyone who required them in Victorian times and this invariably increased the number of deaths from accidental poisoning. Minute quantities of poisons have been part of medical preparations in modern medicine for many years now, although in the nineteenth century when it was more difficult to detect toxin in the body, premeditated poisoning proved a popular form of murder.

Medically speaking, poisons are substances injurious to the organs or tissues of the body, and are classified according to the type of substance that produces the effect. Strong acids or alkalis, for instance, are known as corrosive poisons and burn the tissues, whilst hypnotic poisons include analgesic drugs. Lead, arsenic and mercury derivatives are classed as irritant poisons; strychnine, prussic acid and cyanide of potassium are convulsants; belladonna and chloroform are deliriants, and so on.

(*Left*) Martin's Patent aqua poison; (*right*) narrow-waisted cobalt poison (*Line drawing by Norman Stockton*)

Travelling medicine chest complete with ground glass stoppered bottles, c 1850 (*Courtesy Lea & Perrins Limited*)

Assorted dark green poisons, tallest 17½cm (*Author's collection*)

With so many poisons available, Victorians began to demand safe-guards and to welcome innovations designed to cut down the risks of liquid and crystallised poisons being mistakenly taken as internal medicines. Bottles with lockable stoppers similar to those used for spirits were suggested and discarded as too expensive. Unusually shaped poison bottles fared little better, thus making 'submarines', Martin's 'cut-away' (which gave a measured dosage), 'skull and crossbones' and 'waisted' containers rare and much sought after by today's collectors.

Many rank and file Victorians, it must be remembered, were unable to read and found it difficult to see properly anyway in homes with inadequate lighting. So the need arose for tactile embellishments which would provide universal recognition through sight and touch. Deep vertical ribbing and raised projections seem to have been considered a satisfactory solution to the problem for, together with an embossed warning, this method of recognition has survived into the twentieth century.

The employment of coloured glass was also a successful visual aid to the prevention of death or serious illness resulting from imbibing harmful liquids. The rich, deep blue glass often used for poisons was achieved by adding cobalt to the mix, whilst a lighter blue could be attained through the addition of copper oxide. But whereas most glass bottles prior to 1920 contained manganese and were aqua or light green in colour, dark greens, dark browns and blacks were the end product of increasing the amount of iron oxide in the preparation.

During the early years of Victoria's reign the family chemist tended to make up his own potions in the back room of his premises. At this time medicines were sold in plain glass bottles usually with advertising hand-outs tied around them with string. Traditional herbalism still flourished in most parts of the country, and even as late as the 1860s the young Jesse Boot was known to be working in his mother's herbalist shop in Nottingham. As a boy, Jesse collected herbs, and was educated early in the business of preparing remedies for all kinds of ailments. Prior to the 1860s, of course, there were no anaesthetics or antiseptics and medical men still depended very much on the somewhat drastic measures of purgatives and leechings. The use of herbs by the Victorians was sometimes illustrated by novelists of the period. Mary Ann Evans writing under the name of George Eliot mentions the embittered hand-loom weaver, Silas Marner, searching the fields around the village of Raveloe for foxgloves, dandelions and coltsfoot. A drug (now known as digitalis) was prepared from the dried leaves of foxgloves and used as a heart stimulant, whilst the dried leaves of the dandelion were deemed good for liver complaints and as blood cleansers, the words 'Dandelion Essence' being embossed on numerous Victorian medicine bottles. A syrup was made from coltsfoot by boiling the fresh tops of the herb with sugar and water. It was used as a demulcent for asthma and coughs. The Brontë sisters (Charlotte, Emily and Anne) often collected herbs when out walking on the moors beyond Haworth, and it seems as though their dissipated brother, Branwell, was possibly addicted to the narcotic drug opium. The substance was prepared from the dried exudation of the unripe capsules of the poppy and was used by Victorians as a pain-killer. Charlotte's friend and fellow writer, Elizabeth Gaskell, mentions the gathering of wild herbs in her first novel, *Mary Barton*, published in 1848. These included nettles which, when their leaves were boiled, proved effective as hair conditioners. 'Confection of Nettle-flowers', sold by herbalists and chemists in small earthenware pots, was made by boiling fresh nettle flowers with sugar and water. The liquid was evaporated until the mixture developed the consistency of a conserve. It was then used as an anti-scorbutic.

One of the most successful Victorian vendors of ointments and pills was Thomas Holloway who, when he died at Penzance in 1883, was thought to have assets well in excess of £5 million. 'Professor' Holloway was thirty-eight years of age when he decided to embark on the manufacture of patent medicines and, like other very successful businessmen of the day, was quick to realise the importance of advertising. His ointments, according to his public announcements, could readily cure every illness known to mankind, and by the 1870s he was investing over £40,000 a year on advertising his products. An investment it proved to be, too, for it brought him extremely favourable profits.

The first pots containing Holloway's 'Universal Ointment' ('It mends the legs of men and tables equally well' was one incredible claim) had paper stickers, for although monochrome transfer printing was indeed available by the 1850s, it was not until the 1860s that Holloway adopted this type of underglaze-printed container. His ointment for the cure of gout and rheumatism had a picture of a mother and child on its earthenware container, and also claimed to be a cure for 'inveterate ulcers, sore breasts, sore heads, bad legs' etc.

Thomas Beecham had built a pharmaceutical empire by the 1880s. Like Holloway, Beecham did not enter into the business of pharmacy until his late thirties when he began advertising his famous pills as being 'worth a guinea a box'. His red pills were for the stomach and to purify the blood, whilst those which were green in colour were specifically for back and bladder complaints. Both types, in actual fact, contained soap and a small amount of aperient (usually aloes) which acted as a mild purgative. This gentle action often removed pains in the back and stomach as claimed, for they were probably caused by over-eating and stodgy food. A laxative was all that was needed.

The Nottingham druggist, Jesse Boot, opened his first chemist's shop in 1877, and within six years owned ten branches. His technique of mass selling at reduced prices introduced the modern chain store, which numbered more than 1,000 branches at his death. In 1892, Boot began large-scale manufacture of drugs and by the beginning of the Edwardian era was controlling the largest pharmaceutical retail trade in the world. The last fifteen to twenty years of the nineteenth century saw the take-over of many well known Victorian chemists' groups by Boot, and numerous local brand names were retained and distributed on a much larger scale throughout the chain. Shops acquired in the Norwich area, for instance, now introduced bottles of Cambell's 'Cherry Cough Cure', Dr Armstrong's 'Influenza Mixture' and pots of Girard's 'Glycerine, Cucumber and Honey Cream' to a much wider audience. Others included J. Collis Brown's 'Chlorodyne', a popular pain-soother composed of chloroform, prussic acid and Indian hemp; Smedley's 'Chilly Paste', a vapour rub for the chest; Allen's 'Hair Restorer' at 3s 6d ($17\frac{1}{2}$p) a bottle in the 1880s, and Woodhouse's 'Rheumatic Elixir' at 2s 6d ($12\frac{1}{2}$p) per bottle. These and many more sold alongside Boot's 'Patent Lobelia Pills' for asthma, indigestion and spasms, advertised as 'Health for a shilling'. This was one of Jesse's father's original remedies from the days when he ran his herbalist shop. The lobelia plant (named after Matthias de Lobel, botanist to James I) grew wild in the Nottinghamshire countryside, and Boot senior used its dried leaves as an ingredient of asthma powder which his wife then made into pills by hand. Another of the firm's popular lines was Boot's 'Egg Julep', a hair preparation made from a solution of soap and potassium carbonate in water. The 'egg' content was enterprisingly concocted from water-soluble yellow dye, giving a reasonable imitation of eggs.

At one time there were quack's stalls in every market, but as competition from retailing chemists and druggists increased through price-cutting, so the mountebanks were forced to fight back with blanket-advertising and mail order.

The early nineteenth century had witnessed a massive increase in fraudulent medicine sales, and ignorant pretenders to medicinal skills flourished. Being far from ignorant when it came to selling their spurious products, however, many of these charlatans exploited advertising in such a way that they soon became extremely wealthy individuals. Possibly the best known of these purveyors of quack medicines was Englishman, Thomas William Dyott, who emigrated to Philadelphia in 1805 and there awarded himself a doctorate. Within two years of his arrival in the United States, Dyott's patent cures (under the generic title 'Dr Robertson's Family Medicines') had swept the eastern sea-board, although many of his remedies had been 'borrowed' from their original owners and inventors across the Atlantic.

Initially, the wily 'Doctor' imported unembossed containers from England, preferring what he considered to be 'these superior bottles and jars' to their American counterparts. Because of commercial disputes arising out of the conflict with Napoleon in Europe, however, America fought a war with England between 1812 and 1814 which resulted in the British capturing and burning Washington. During this period, Dyott's supplies of imported medicines were almost completely cut off, with only the odd case penetrating the blockades at night. But far from putting him out of business, the embargo determined Dyott to reproduce popular British medicine bottles and fill them with his own mixtures. Having bought into a local glass-works, he was soon turning out excellent copies of Dicey & Co's 'True Daffy's Elixir', Dalby's 'Carminative' and Robert Turlington's odd-shaped 'Balsam of Life', and by 1820 he owned his own works. During the next fifteen to twenty years, Dyott became a very rich man, his particular brand of charlatanism paving the way for others to continue throughout the nineteenth century.

It was almost certainly due to the fact that the Victorian era was so free from advertising restrictions that tricksters in the Dyott mould prospered. Quite outrageous and amusing claims accompanied practically every remedy on the market, to the extent that if only half of them proved to be true, many Victorians would still be alive today. There were pills, lotions, creams, emulsions, ointments and substances of all kinds for headaches, fevers, baldness, spots, pimples, sores, deafness, colds, coughs, rheumatics, gout, piles, feet, bladder, stomach, lungs, kidneys, heart, eyes, teeth, gums – in fact a cure for every ailment. The ideal age, it would seem, to be ill in. Cure-alls had flooded the market by the 1870s, a typical example being Vogeler's 'Curative Compound', the company belonging to Charles A. Vogeler, in London's Farringdon Road. The compound was made from perfectly harmless vegetable oils 'prepared in England by English people', and was stated to be a positive cure for every form of dyspepsia, liver complaint, kidney disease, indigestion, acidity, sleeplessness, weakness, nervousness, languor, debility, melancholia, hysteria, anaemia, head-ache, heartburn, dizziness, ringing noises in the head, eczema, and all diseases arising from impure blood and stomach disorders.

The company's motto, oddly enough, was 'Vogeler's Cures', and the product carried the following warning:

Beware of foreign imitators who attempt to convey our style of advertising by using some of our most prominent phrases. Insist on having Vogeler's, which bears the fac-simile signature of the proprietors.

As was fashionable with proprietors of cure-alls, Vogeler's had many 'testimonials' on hand to enforce their extravagant claims. A letter dating from the 1880s and purporting to have come from a Mr J. A. Moston of Durham, says that the writer had been afflicted with dyspepsia since 1879. He was often bloated, had offensive breath, distress and pain in his stomach, and had spent over £100 trying to get cured. In spite of this, the affliction had grown steadily worse, until he had taken Vogeler's, which had made him well. 'I took six bottles; I am a new man.'

If we find it difficult to understand why people could be so easily

Warner's 'Safe Cure' bottles in amber, tallest 24cm (*Author's collection*)

cheated, it might be considered that the ordinary Victorians had no National Health Service to rely on, and could in no way afford the expensive medical services available. In illness, their only hope lay with the dozens of cure-alls or elixirs available at local chemist's shops, many of which were worthless potions claiming to work miracles.

The majority of patent medicine bottles found in Victorian dumps are quite common but Warner's 'Safe Remedies', although familiar to collectors and diggers, are considered scarce in Britain. These bottles, in amber-brown and olive-green, are regularly found in North American dumps for they were designed to package the quack medicines of H. H. Warner & Co of Rochester, New York, from 1879 through to the 1930s. The company was founded by Hulbert H. Warner who, at an earlier date, had been well known as a manufacturer of safes. Thus Warner's 'Safe Remedies' was a natural choice for his patent medicines. Warner used a safe as his trade mark and embossed the words 'Safe Cure' on all his bottles. The venture proved so successful that establishments were soon opened in London, Melbourne, Toronto, Frankfurt, and Pressburgh, Austria, which is now the Czechoslovakian city of Bratislava. The word 'Rochester', 'London', 'Melbourne' or 'Frankfurt' was embossed beneath the safe trade mark according to the bottle's point of sale. No containers bearing the word 'Toronto' or 'Pressburgh' have yet been found and it is unlikely that they ever will be, for these office-warehouses were almost certainly supplied by Rochester and Frankfurt respectively. The company marketed 'Safe Cure', 'Kidney and Liver Cure', 'Rheumatic Cure', 'Nervine', 'Diabetes Cure' and 'Compound' mainly in pint and half-pint sizes, the green and amber bottles having a thickish 'hump' base and sloping shoulders.

Warner's 'Safe Cure' advertisements claimed complete cure for 'Bright's Disease' (an inflammation of the kidneys), urinary disorders, female disorders, female complaints, general debility, malaria and all diseases caused by disordered kidneys and livers. Later analysis by the United States Government, revealed that the mixture was in fact little more than coloured water. Warner eventually sold his interest in the business in 1884 and the company had sold out completely within ten years to the Duffy Company, distillers of pure malt whiskey, although it continued under its famous trade name and is listed in Rochester directories through until 1934.

Another New England cure-all sold successfully in Britain was William Radam's 'Microbe Killer'. This amber container is rare to Victorian dumps and has an embossed front panel depicting a skeleton (symbolising disease) under attack, and the words 'Germ, bacteria & fungus destroyer – cures all diseases'. This trade mark was registered on 13 December 1887. Here again, government analysis found the nostrum to be comprised mainly of water and acid. Rooke's 'Solar Elixir and Reanimating Balm of Life', Dr Rooke's cobalt blue 'Rheumatic Lixine', the wedge-shaped Silby's 'Solar Tincture', the so-called blood purifier in its dark-green bottle known as 'Dr Townsend's Sarsaparilla', Fenner's 'Kidney and Backache Cure' and many more such remedies of doubtful content all successfully aided quack medicine manufacturers on both sides of the Atlantic to hood-wink a gullible public.

Mention should be made, however, of the fact that some of the largest pharmaceutical houses now in existence had their origins in small herbalist's or nostrum hawkers and have, in the long term, done much to benefit society. The Beecham Group through their modern research laboratories, for example, have produced new synthetic penicillins, alleviating suffering throughout the world; Jesse Boot donated over £1,000,000 to Nottingham University and as much again to the city itself; even the famous Victorian quack, Thomas Holloway,

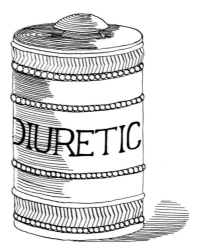

Doulton decorated brown stoneware druggist's pot (*Line drawing by Norman Stockton*)

was induced to spend some of his fortune near Virginia Water in Surrey, where he founded London University's Holloway College for women.

Some good, too, was derived from patent medicines containing empirically discovered drugs, and recent pharmaceutical research has shown that although many were useless or only mildly beneficial, others had great potential. Quinine, for instance, is the chief alkaloid in cinchona bark and was used by Peruvian indians as a fever cure. It was introduced to Europe in 1639 as a treatment for the ague, but was not identified by pure chemistry until the second quarter of the nineteenth century when it was 'discovered' and named by French chemists, Pierre Pelletier and Joseph Caventou. Later it was used to kill the blood parasites causing malaria, but has now been supplanted by the less toxic and more powerful synthetics such as chloroquine.

The common cold has been with us for some considerable time now, but although a minor disease caused by a variety of viruses, little seems to have been done to prevent it. In Victorian times, as now, there were untold remedies available to the suffering public – although the words 'guaranteed to ease' rather than 'guaranteed to cure' are carefully inserted in the advertising rubric of today.

The Victorian cold sufferer was lucky; he could venture forth and purchase a wealth of medicinal compounds which were 'certain to cure' his cold, cough or sore throat. Bottles and jars lining the shelves of chemist's shops would have included 'Pectoral Ointment' (containing oil of sweet almonds, chamomile and violet flowers, chicken's and duck's fats, orris root, saffron and white wax); 'Syrup of Myrtle' (boiled myrtle flowers, sugar and distilled water); 'Glycerine

Late nineteenth-century medicine bottles. (*Left to right*) J. C. Eno's 'Effervescing Fruit Salt', 16½cm; Scott's 'Emulsion' (Cod Liver Oil with Lime & Soda), 19cm; Woodward's 'Gripe Water', 15cm; Veno's 'Lightning Cough Cure', 12½cm; (*foreground*) Dr Sage's 'Catarrh Remedy', Buffalo, U. S. A. 6cm (*Author's collection*)

and Horehound Cough Elixir'; 'Pectakos'; J. Collis Browne's 'Chlorodyne' ('a few doses will cure all incipient cases'); Kay's 'Linseed Cough Compound' (Kay Brothers of Stockport were chemists and druggists to Queen Victoria from June 1884); Walter Thomas Owbridge's 'Lung Tonic' (Owbridge was Sheriff of Hull around the turn of the century); Cundell's 'Improved Balsam of Honey'; Ford's 'Pectoral Balsam of Horehound'; Roche's 'Herbal Embrocation' (4s (20p) a bottle, for whooping cough); 'Bovril' ('the resisting power required to protect you from an attack of influenza'), and hundreds more.

Rather interesting were the small, glass-stoppered smelling bottles to relieve blocked nasal passages. Dr Mackenzie's 'Catarrh Cure' in its tiny cylindrical container of dark-green glass was accompanied by the following statement:

100 Guineas reward will be paid to any person who can prove that Dr Mackenzie's Catarrh Cure has not Cured Nervous Headache in a few minutes, Cold in the Head in a few hours, or Instantly Relieved Hay Fever and Neuralgic pains in the face.

An American contemporary of Dr Mackenzie was Dr V. M. Pierce of Buffalo, New York – 'The people's common-sense medical adviser in plain English'. Pierce marketed 'Dr Sage's Catarrh Remedy' in tiny bottles with sloping shoulders, and these aqua containers have been found in both British and American nineteenth-century dumps.

If the common cold defied a cure, so too did baldness. In truth the exact causes of baldness were not known, although there were many claims that certain remedies could produce improvement or indeed a complete cure. The common, patterned type of baldness is now thought to be hereditary and totally resistent to treatment, being transmitted via women to their sons. The condition was associated, in certain Victorian circles, with the development of secondary sexual characteristics, the only prevention being castration. Eunuchs having undergone this operation prior to being functionally capable of procreation apparently never went bald, but it seemed that the majority of balding Victorian men preferred to put their faith in the medicines available rather than succumb to this somewhat drastic and painful 'treatment'.

Victorians were extremely sensitive not only to loss of hair but also to loss of hair colour, and there were many popular preparations available. Seeger's 'Hair Dye' had an annual sale of over 360,000 bottles at the turn of the century, whilst to darken grey hair Lockyer's 'Sulphur Hair Restorer' was claimed to be the quickest, best, safest and cheapest with large bottles selling at 1s 6d ($7\frac{1}{2}$p) each. Rowland's 'Macassar Oil' was supposed to strengthen the hair and prevent it from 'falling off'; 'Koko' was accompanied by many of the usual advertising claims but had the extra bonus of 'being a strong nerve tonic and invigorating to the brain'. It also had the supposed patronage of Her Royal Highness Princess Victoria of Schaumburg-Lippe, granddaughter of Queen Victoria. William Lasson's 'Hair Elixir' was, however, refreshingly honest. Having claimed superiority over all other 'washes' it stated that the mixture 'does not, indeed, possess the property of producing hair where the roots no longer exist – for there is no remedy capable of doing so.'

The firm of Lea & Perrins, of 'Worcestershire Sauce' fame, had developed quite a sizeable home and overseas trade with their proprietary lines by 1850. These evidently included Locock's 'Lotion for the Hair' and 'Marrow Pomade', and a descriptive leaflet from this time throws additional light on the uninhibited advertising copy of those days:

Dr Locock's Lotion will be esteemed as most beneficial in counteracting the pernicious effects of salt water when bathing; and by its daily use, either alone or in conjunction with the MARROW POMADE that healthy state of the Hair will be induced, which must be the object of all who study comfort and personal appearance.

Far more extravagant was the advertisement by Edward's 'Harlene' Company of London. Their product was not only 'world-renowned', it was 'positively the best hairdressing':

Produces luxuriant hair. Prevents it falling off and turning grey. Unequal for promoting the growth of the beard and moustache. The world-renowned remedy for baldness. For curing weak and thin eyelashes, preserving, strengthening, and rendering the hair beautifully soft. For removing scurf and dandruff. For restoring grey hair to its natural colour. IT IS WITHOUT A RIVAL.

Unembossed bottles containing all kinds of herbal remedies for baldness and falling hair were also available at competitive prices. A lotion made from the seeds and leaves of nettles could be used for massaging the scalp and rejuvenating the hair; the dried leaves and stalks of parsley when boiled were claimed to produce a lotion capable of staving off baldness; the young tops, leaves and flowers of rosemary mixed with boiling water and borax supposedly made a splendid hair wash that would clear dandruff, tone and brighten the hair, and prevent premature baldness; yarrow seemingly served a similar purpose.

The Cheltenham pharmacy of Michael Beetham & Son was established in the small Cotswold town's High Street as early as the 1840s, the firm making a name for itself locally with its hair tonic and hair dye preparations. Within a decade it had moved to the now well known premises at 22 Promenade Villas, the address which appears on all Beetham & Son or Beetham & Clarke pot lids reclaimed on digs throughout the British Isles. Being a man of vision, Beetham saw the possibilities of expanding his business far beyond the confines of Gloucestershire. He was quick to observe the tired faces of rich, middle-aged ladies who visited Cheltenham to imbibe of and to bathe in its spa waters. His experiments sought to perfect a preparation that would enhance the complexion, and in 1860 Beetham's 'Glycerine and Cucumber' was introduced successfully to the public. A colourless, viscous, odourless, sweetish liquid, glycerine was ideal for maintaining moist conditions in cosmetics, whilst the fruit of the cucumber was renowned for its cool, soothing and refreshing properties.

Inferior imitations of his lotion forced Beetham to register a similar product under the name of 'Lait Larola' in 1899, and bottles embossed with this and the former name are common to most Victorian dumps of

83

the last quarter of the nineteenth century. M. Beetham & Son also produced 'Rose and Cucumber Cold Cream' and 'Cherry Tooth Paste', the pot lids of which had a distinct diamond pattern encircling the wording. Lids identical to these, but bearing the name Beetham & Clarke, date from 28 April 1905, when a merger took place.

Beetham advertised his products extensively and often out-flanked rivals like Thomasso's 'Royal Complexion Beautifier' by the use of poetry. One such advertisement read:

> Once beauty bore a sunshade large
> To shield her soft white skin,
> And o'er her charming features fair
> An envious veil did pin.
>
> But now in Old Sol's burning rays
> She dares to sweetly slumber,
> For Beetham puts her all to rights
> With Glycerine and Cucumber.

This particular advertisement depicted two Victorian bathing beauties confidently soaking up the sun at the seaside and having, of course, a handy 2s 6d ($12\frac{1}{2}$p) bottle of Beetham's famous lotion well within reach for protection.

Robert Augustus Chesebrough was born in London in the year of Queen Victoria's accession and was later to discover yet another famous name in cosmetics: 'Vaseline' petroleum jelly. His eye-catching 'Vaseline' advertisements were placed on horse-drawn buses and rumbling trams of the late Victorian era, along with those for 'Lipton's Tea', 'Heinz Baked Beans', 'Colman's Mustard', 'Bovril', 'Remington Typewriters' and many more.

The earlier narrow-necked glass jar was embossed CHESEBROUGH VASELINE MANUFACT'G CO and had a laid-on ring to reinforce the neck of the container against the pressure of the cork closure. Writing to the company from Great New Street, London, a letter from Dickens dated 30 January 1862 reads:

Gentlemen,
> I have to thank you for the samples of your Vaseline manufactures of the value of which I have a very high opinion. I'll not fail to mention them should the occasion serve.
> > Faithfully yours,
> > Charles Dickens.

In the final sentence, the great man was probably referring to possible future comments in 'Household Words', a weekly journal founded in 1850 by Dickens and edited by him until his death in 1870.

Laxatives were probably the most effective cure for the many mysterious pains acquired by our Victorian ancestors, and some of these remedies are still in use. Eno's 'Fruit Salt' appears to have originated in Newcastle on Tyne in the early 1870s, but Mr J. C. Eno opened his works at Hatcham, London, on 8 July 1878 and by the mid-eighties employed about fifty people. He was extremely fond of using quotations by famous writers and poets including Pope, Wordsworth and Thackeray – all based on family love, piety and kindliness. A typical quote (from the works of George Eliot) reads:

What do we live for, if not to make life less difficult for each other?

Presumably Eno had his 'Fruit Salt' in mind at the time, for many of the other quotations he employed followed a similar theme.

Allen & Handbury's 'Perfected Cod Liver Oil' and the California Fig Syrup Company's 'Syrup of Figs' provided equally good, if not so lyrical, alternatives, whilst for 6d ($2\frac{1}{2}$p) the Emerson Drug Co Ltd would supply a trial bottle of their 'Bromo-Seltzer' post free. Dinneford's 'Pure Fluid Magnesia' was advertised as the best mild aperient for delicate constitutions, being specially adapted for ladies, children and infants. By 1877 William Woodward, a Nottingham chemist, was preparing and selling Woodward's 'Gripe Water', the medicine having been invented some three years earlier by a Dr Thomas Burnie of Mansfield Road, Nottingham.

These children's medicines must have proved invaluable when one remembers that penny sticks of opium could be bought thirty years earlier for the same purpose. A very high percentage of children died before the age of five, their diet often being so deficient in protein that much pain was suffered from cold, damp, and exhaustion. It was little wonder that babies and small children exposed to such conditions were fretful and cried continually. Working mothers, forced out to work to scrape together a meagre living in the first half of the nineteenth century, frequently gave their babies 'Godfrey's Cordial' to make them sleep. This concoction contained opium and treacle, but many infants were given spirits or laudanum as well. Spirits would warm the stomach of a cold and hungry child, whilst laudanum would sooth a crying baby to sleep. Needless to say, many children died in opium-induced sleep, a common fate for infants too small to work or to be let loose to wander the streets begging.

Victorian medicine boasted cures for most things, so it comes as little surprise that animals were well catered for, too. Luddington's 'Oils for Cattle', Day and Sons 'Black Drink', Vanner and Prest's 'Embrocation for Horses', Elliman's 'Royal Embrocation', Tipper's 'Colic Drink',

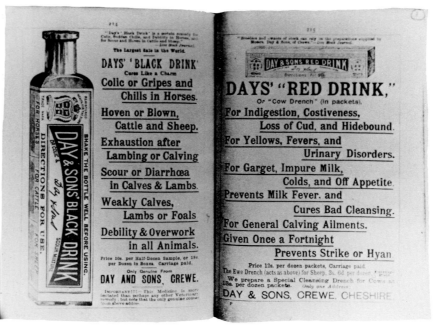

Day & Sons 'Black Drink' advert, c 1890 (*Author's collection*)

were just a few of the wide range of veterinary medicines available in the late 1800s.

The Slough firm of Elliman attributed much of their early success to a combination of the excellence of their embrocation (for stiffness, aches, sprains and bruises) and a policy of devoting half their profits to advertising. Elliman's 'Universal Embrocation' was first introduced about 1847, the firm's famous product being beneficial to human beings as well as to animals. Because horses and cattle tended to use up more embrocation than people, Elliman's also sold their 'Royal Embrocation' in 10s 6d (52½p) and 20s (£1) 'economical' glass jars, for cash only.

The business remained in the Elliman family until it was acquired by Horlicks Limited at the beginning of 1961, but continued to operate under its own name. Horlicks is now part of the giant Beecham Group, who continue to manufacture pharmaceuticals for human and veterinary use, but Elliman's 'Embrocation' is no longer made.

One of the largest Victorian firms manufacturing and selling animal medicines and embrocations was Day and Sons of Crewe in Cheshire. The firm was founded at Shavington near Crewe in 1840, moving to Crewe in the 1860s. Farmers swore by the validity of Day's famous 'Black Drink' which 'cures like a charm' colic or gripes and chills in horses; hoven or blown cattle and sheep; exhaustion after lambing or

(*Left*) Vanner & Prest's 'Embrocation for Horses', 16cm including stopper; (*right*) Elliman's 'Royal Embrocation for Horses', 19½cm including stopper (*Author's collection*)

(*Far right*) Elliman's 'Universal Embrocation' advert, late nineteenth century (*Author's collection*)

calving; scour or diarrhoea in calves and lambs; weakly calves, lambs or foals; debility and overwork in all animals. Day's 'Red Drink' was a cow drench sold in packets, but their 'Huskolein' for tapeworms and internal parasitic animal disorders came in bottles costing 6s 6d (32½p) each. An antiseptic for soothing all wounds in all animals, Day's 'Purified Driffield Oils' could be purchased in large 6s (30p) bottles, but smaller containers were available if required.

In common with human medicine bottles, animal preparations of the kind mentioned are fairly prevalent in most Victorian dumps, but are interesting for their comparisons with human cure-alls, ointments and the like.

6
PERFUME AND INK BOTTLES

A marked increase in the general prosperity of Victorians in the second half of the nineteenth century did much to widen the scope of English perfume manufacturers. At last the bourgeoisie were in a position to demand a share in luxury commodities previously confined to the very wealthy, thus encouraging a number of notable perfume houses to make the transition from modest shops to sizeable factories and laboratories.

The advent of mass-production techniques enabled the individual perfumer to offer his services to a much wider public than ever before. This factor, coupled with greater advertising facilities and know-how, quickly rendered his products acceptable to a whole new stratum of Victorian society.

Possibly the most widely known of English perfumers founded in the nineteenth century was The House of Yardley. William Yardley was the first member of the family to own the enterprise, trading in the 1820s as a sword-cutler and as a supplier of lavender, soap and cosmetics. By 1851, the firm was exhibiting at the Great Exhibition in the Crystal Palace, whilst the *Druggists' Circular* of January 1879 revealed that Yardley soaps were being exported to the United States of America in no less than twenty-two varieties. A joint stock company was created in 1890 with a capital of £172,000, and within the first decade of the twentieth century Yardley & Co Ltd had become recognised as one of the world's leading soap and perfumery houses.

Yardley perfume bottles came in a variety of sizes, shapes and colours, were usually unembossed, had stoppers of ground glass, and contained (among others) the firm's 'Old English Lavender', 'Eau de Cologne', 'Moon Flower' and 'Enchantress' toilet waters and perfumes. As Yardley & Statham, the firm were also selling 'Genuine Bears Grease' in small earthenware pots in the 1850s and 1860s. The lids of these containers carried a picture of a bear and beehive, together with the words 'Genuine Bear's Grease Yardley & Statham Wholesale Perfumers'. A rarer specimen of Yardley's bear's grease, was a lid depicting a large bear with a chain in its mouth, this container once being packed with 'Imperial

Perfume bottles of late nineteenth century and early twentieth century (*Courtesy Yardley & Company Limited*)

Russian Bear's Grease', perfumed with attar of roses. A rare Yardley's toothpaste lid from the 1890s had underglaze decoration comprising red cherries and green leaves. Some of these rectangular lids have an onglaze ornamental border and blue band around the edges, whilst some have only a plain border.

Apparently the Victorian perfume industry was not without its fair share of counterfeiters. Imitations, passed off as genuine, again forced manufacturers to issue cautions to the public stressing the authenticity of their products. An example of this was issued from Cologne in February 1873:

> Caution – Eau de Cologne – Mr. Johann Maria Farina, opposite the Julich's Place, Cologne, sole purveyor to Her Majesty Queen Victoria and their Royal Highnesses the Prince and Princess of Wales, begs to caution the public against spurious imitations of Eau de Cologne. His label, which has never been altered, bears his name and address as below, without the addition of any number, in black letters on a plain white ground – Johann Maria Farina, Gegenüber dem Julich's Platz. It can be obtained of all respectable firms dealing in perfumery.

Consisting of a solution of volatile oils in alcohol, it is perhaps hardly surprising that Eau de Cologne was often mixed with wine or spirits and drunk. Indeed it was held to be a certain cure for a hangover when mixed with Rochelle-salt (a tartrate of soda and potash, used as Epsom salt), an infusion of senna and a teaspoon of tincture of cardamom (an Indian spice).

The London perfumers, H. Labern & Son, who became established in Bouverie Street in 1841, were also honoured by the patronage of Queen Victoria. Towards the end of the nineteenth century their 'perfumes of highest excellence', including a distinctive perfume known as 'Flower of France', were selling at prices ranging from 2s 6d (12½p) to 8s (40p) per bottle. Elegant cut glass bottles could also be purchased from the firm as gifts in fancy cases from 10s 6d (52½p), 15s (75p), 21s (£1.05) and 30s (£1.50) each.

Murray & Lanman's 'Florida Water', a perfume resembling Eau de Cologne, was widely advertised as 'the universal perfume' for handkerchief, toilet and bath, whilst the Medico-Hygienic Inventions Co Ltd sold its 'Lance Perfumes' in sprays from London's Queen Victoria Street. Spray containers such as these were usually displayed on dressing tables along with cold creams, pomades, Circassian Creams (Circassian women from the Northern Caucasus in Russia were prized by Turkish merchants for the harems of the East because of their remarkable beauty), lip salves and the like.

The natural aromatic materials used in perfumes in Victorian times were blended from flowers, leaves, fruits, seeds, roots, resins, woods and barks. The odours from these were held captive by natural animal fixatives. The town of Grasse in Southern France became quite important to nineteenth-century perfumers, for the terrain surrounding it produced (and still produces) tons of orange blossom, roses and violets from which the essence was extracted to make some of the finest scents. The lavender fields of Norfolk, England, provided some of the finest lavender oil in the world; Asia produced various scented sandalwoods; Oriental styrax or sweet-gum trees yielded storax, a resinous vanilla-scented balsam much used in Victorian perfumes; patchouli, an Indian plant, contained a fragrant oil from which perfume was prepared, and so on. Fixative and diluting agents used in nineteenth-century perfumery included alcohol from molasses or grain, but the finest perfumes came from a skilful blending of many substances.

An import from Russia in the early 1800s was bear's grease which was used in pomades. Victorian pomades were scented ointments for the hair and skin of the head. James Atkinson, founder of the Bond Street perfumers, even had a tame bear chained to the wall of his first shop in Soho to attract customers into purchasing his pomades, soaps and perfumes. He imported his grease from St Petersburg, and packed it in small circular pots with a basic design of a muzzled and chained bear on the lid. This illustration, together with the Old Bond Street address and the price mark of 2s 6d ($12\frac{1}{2}$p) is the most commonly found of Victorian bear's grease lids, and a great many dating from the last two decades of the nineteenth century have been retrieved from dumps all over England. On its own, bear's grease quickly turned rancid, but the young Atkinson astutely perfumed the fat with attar of roses, thus producing a pomatum which became extremely popular.

As the business prospered, other lines were added including Atkinson's 'Vegetable Dye' and 'Mahomed's Turkish Dye' for the hair, 'Old Windsor' and 'Ambrosial' soaps, various shaving pastes and cakes, 'Rose Cold Cream' for the hands, depilatories (applications for removing superfluous hair without damaging the skin), and permanent ink. Many of these products were being sold in chemists' shops throughout Britain by the 1870s.

So unrivalled in quality were the perfumes sold by James Atkinson, that by 1826 he was perfumer to the Royal Family, and five years later formed a partnership with his brother, Edward. His first major success as Court Perfumer was probably with 'Persian Bouquet de Rose', which was specially made for the Atkinson establishment by a distillery at Grasse. The classic 'Eau de Cologne' was also imported initially, but from Prussia, where the Farina family had had their business from the beginning of the eighteenth century. This world-famous scent contained attar of neroli (an oil distilled from the flowers of the bitter Seville orange), essence of rosemary, and a greenish-tinted attar obtained from the rind of the pear-shaped bergamot fruit. These were then dissolved in spirit. Cognac, for example, because it was made from the distilled extract of grapes from that district and thus had a characteristic odour, gave what many regarded as the *true* Eau de Cologne its very special fragrance.

Atkinson's 'Essence of Lavender' proved much stronger than its continental rivals, and was free from fixatives such as ambergris or musk. A fixative in perfumery terms, of course, was a liquid that retarded evaporation. Ambergris, for example, a grey excretory product of the sperm whale, was soluble in alcohol and had the means of enhancing and retaining the scent of attars with which it was blended. The odour of ambergris resembled that of a resinous substance that exuded from the leaves and twigs of various kinds of cistus or rock-roses, but was only employed in the preparation of the more expensive perfumes due to its high cost.

Musk was another very expensive and powerful fixative used in perfumes of Victorian times, having such a penetrating odour that the East India Company flatly refused to include it in its tea shipments. Obtained from the male musk-deer, musk-ox and musk-rat, musk was a

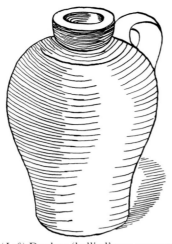 

(*Left*) Doulton 'bellied' two-ounce stoneware scent bottle (*Line drawing by Norman Stockton*)

Doulton 'upright' two-ounce stoneware scent bottle (*Line drawing by Norman Stockton*)

sex gland secretion of waste products which, like the secretion of the civet cat (a similar fixative), was rather unpleasant in its unadulterated form. On its own, the odour of a perfume could evaporate quite rapidly, and thus required a fixative such as musk to replace the wax or resin present in the flower or leaf from which the essence was extracted. When adulterated, musk had a sweet smell similar to that of honey, the finest supposedly coming from the mountainous province of Szechuen in Western China where, just below the snow line, the deer ate juniper and other such herbs from which the odour was in part derived.

Although fixatives such as musk, civet and ambergris were considerably expensive, perfumers could and often did use gums and resins for this purpose. Oils of cedar-wood and sandalwood, for instance, as well as being much cheaper to use than animal fixatives, blended admirably with the attars and provided them with a less ephemeral quality.

It is perhaps interesting to note whilst on the subject of fixatives, that Josephine, Empress of France, was so partial to the scent of musk that she had her dressing-room at her favourite residence, La Malmaison, perfumed with it daily. The unmistakeable redolence remains to this day, a haunting reminder of an accomplished Creole lady from Martinique who died over one hundred and sixty years ago. Napoleon, too, was appreciative of perfumes, especially the cooling properties of Eau de Cologne, which contained the scent of rosemary so familiar to his native Corsica. Although having been divorced from Josephine for five years when she died in 1814, Napoleon had her grave covered with violets, her favourite flowers. When he died some seven years later, the locket he always wore around his neck was found to contain these violets together with her portrait.

Glass stoppered scent bottles with Crown Perfumery Company bottle, 7¾cm, on right
(Author's collection)

Some fifty or so years after Bonaparte's death, a fellow Corsican and lover of fine scents, François Coty, was born at Ajaccio. As a young man he gleaned much of his knowledge of perfumes from a chemist friend in Paris and also at first hand in the flower fields of Grasse, so that by the turn of the century he was successfully marketing his exquisite rose bouquet in leading Paris stores. His idea of presenting perfumes in fine French crystal containers proved a shrewd one, with bottles by glass craftsmen such as Lalique becoming almost as sought after as the scents they contained.

Some very fine examples of Irish Waterford glass scent bottles from the nineteenth century still exist in reasonable numbers, as do the blue jasper scent containers of Josiah Wedgwood; but a great deal of good fortune would be required to unearth such items of value in Victorian rubbish dumps. Works of art in their own right, these containers would have been handed down from generation to generation, and the possibility of any of them having been thrown away intact would be very remote indeed.

Possibly half way between the exotic and the plain versions of the Victorian scent container might be placed those of the Crown Perfumery Co of London. All the bottles issued by this company had crown-shaped stoppers, this unusual type of closure being registered as the trade mark of the firm. The company had various London addresses between 1870 and 1900, including manufacturing premises in Bow, a bonded stores at Red Lion Wharf, Upper Thames Street, and wholesale and retailing outlets in Cheapside and New Bond Street.

Crown Perfumery was advertising its products extensively by the 1880s, one of their most sought after lines being 'Crown Violet Perfume'. The violet was in commercial cultivation in Greece over two thousand years before its scent became a favourite with Victorians, and was even the symbol of the city of Athens. In the nineteenth century it was believed that the violet lost its fragrance when cut, but it was a ketone known as ionone which caused the flower's perfume and thus its strange 'evaporating' quality. This affected the olfactory nerves in that the more the violet's scent was inhaled, the more rapidly it faded, the sense of smell being caused to malfunction temporarily.

A typical late nineteenth-century press advertisement by Crown Perfumes, was for their 'Lavender Salts' which were 'genuine only in Crown stoppered bottles'. These popular smelling salts could also be used as a deodoriser, so that by leaving the stopper out for a few moments, a delightful perfume was allowed to escape and presumably 'freshen' the air. The company's pots of 'Cold Cream of Roses' also bore the crown trade mark on their lids and were printed in red with the full company address within a decorative border.

A 'delicious new perfume' from Crown in the 1890s was their 'Crabb Apple Blossoms', claimed to be the only scent of its kind available. But although perhaps new to Victorians, the scent of apples was once believed to be extremely refreshing to the mind. The peoples of Southern Greece had made unguents from the fruit for many years before the birth of Christ, the best perfume from apples in those days reputedly coming from Cos, one of the fertile Dodecanese islands in the Aegean Sea.

The House of Floris was yet another fashionable Victorian perfumery, having been established by a Minorcan, Juan Floris, in the 1730s. The firm was situated in London's Jermyn Street, and had gained a royal warrant from George IV as early as 1821. A Floris catalogue from the 1860s indicates the patronage of Queen Victoria, for it bears her royal cipher. Makers of combs, and perfumers to royalty, their famous smelling salts came in glass bottles with patent stoppers and were filled with absorbent material soaked in scented ammonia. Eau de Cologne by Floris came in wickered glass containers and, like the Atkinson Perfumery, was supplied from Cologne by the firm of Farina.

Closely linked with the Victorian perfumery industry, was snuff manufacture, for this powdered preparation of tobacco was invariably scented with attars of all kinds. Attar was a general term used by perfumers to indicate an oil distilled from the petals of flowers – particularly roses. Bulgaria's Valley of Roses, for example, had long been famous for its production of attar of roses, approximately 350 of the flowers being required to supply a pound of petals. Having been mixed with water and distilled in large vats, the oil was skimmed off after various processes, some thousands of petals contributing to the making of as little as two drops of attar.

As with cut glass perfumes, silver- and pewter-mounted smelling bottles and the like, Victorian snuff containers seldom come to light in old refuse dumps, although a few have been discovered in this manner in recent years.

By mid-century, glass works had found a profitable outlet in manufacturing containers for a whole range of chemists' sundries including poisons, disinfectants, smelling salts, pomades and perfumes. Some of the larger retailing chemists even bought into or took over glass-making concerns in order to dictate more precisely the types of bottles, jars and vials they required. Mustard, pepper, pickles, varnish, glue, snuff and oil could also be purchased from the Victorian chemist, as could writing fluids in various colours together with packets of writing sand. The beginning of the Victorian era saw chemists making and selling their own ink, although it could still be obtained in powdered form – a legacy from the previous century.

The introduction of the pre-paid penny post in the United Kingdom in 1840 by Rowland Hill contributed significantly to an increased demand for ink, as prior to the January of that year letters had had to be paid for by the recipient on a rate which varied according to distance – an often costly experience. Quill and reed pens were becoming out-dated by this time, and were being replaced with steel-nibbed rivals. Joseph Bramah, a Yorkshireman who distinguished himself by the number, value and ingenuity of his inventions, contributed greatly to this transition when he introduced a machine for cutting up the quill into three or four lengths and then splitting these up into blanks. This lame cabinet-maker had, in 1809, succeeded in producing an ingenious cutting tool not only capable of saving many hours of labour (for the shaping of quill pens, although exacting, was a constant necessity) but also of creating uniformity. Indeed it was through Bramah's invention that people became acquainted with the use of a nib slipped into a holder (as with the steel pen).

Josiah Mason began making steel pens for James Perry & Co of London in 1828. Perry, in a patent of 1830, ambitiously sought to make

Doulton and Lovatt & Lovatt stoneware bulk inks, tallest 15cm (*Author's collection*)

steel pens more flexible by cutting a centre hole between the points and the shoulders and cutting one or more slits on each side of the centre slit, but it was Mason who soon became the greatest pen-maker in the world. Before his death in 1881, he had endowed almshouses and an orphanage at a cost of £260,000 and given £180,000 to found Mason College which is now Birmingham University.

The steel pens manufactured by John Mitchell at his Newhall Street Works in Birmingham were patronised by Queen Victoria from the late 1840s onwards, Her Majesty being able to write fluently with either hand. A contemporary of Perry, Mitchell gained much of the credit for introducing machine-made pens, although James Perry was known to have been working along similar lines at much the same time.

Another Birmingham-based manufacturer of steel-nibbed pens was Joseph Gillot who, along with Mason, shared the credit of having perfected the making of steel pens and, like Mitchell, was pen manufacturer to Victoria. Within two years of Hill's penny post, Gillot's Midlands factory was producing 70 million pens every twelve months in an attempt to provide for the great surge of letter-writing brought about by the new mail delivery system.

The sale of ink, of course, was equally spectacular, fluid ink quickly replacing the powdered form towards the middle of the nineteenth

Assorted glass inks of late nineteenth century with sheared lips, tallest 8cm. Note ink with pen rest shoulders on right (*Author's collection*)

century. Stoneware bottles were used to sell writing fluid, liquid blacking and other similar commodities by the pint, and dozens of these containers are being unearthed regularly at Victorian dumps throughout Britain. Many are quite attractive in their own way, having matt or gloss finishes in glazes varying from light to reddish and dark brown to grey and off-white. The Denby Pottery of Joseph Bourne made vast quantities of bulk ink containers, many finding their way into collections throughout the world. At least four different marks used by the Denby Pottery can be found incised on the sides of their Derbyshire produced range of bottles, depending upon their date and place of manufacture. The matt-finished bulk inks of Lovatt & Lovatt from Langley Mill, Nottinghamshire, are usually incised near the base, possess a pouring lip, and have a rich lustreless reddish glaze which lends itself admirably to bottle displays. The majority of Victorian stoneware inks had cork closures and bore some evidence of labelling, a few even having spouts and handles.

Doulton's of Lambeth manufactured large quantities of ink bottles and inkwells over a long period, beginning as early as 1815 and extending into the 1930s. Possibly their largest customer was the famous London firm of Henry Stephens who, by the 1840s, was selling Stephens' 'Writing Fluid' in 'the most splendid and durable colours'. The Lambeth pottery also supplied stoneware ink containers to the Admiralty, the War Office, the Board of Education, and other government departments, as well as to universities, colleges, schools and other institutions. These were made in a variety of shapes and sizes, in plain brown, cream and sometimes blue-coloured stoneware, some having the customer's name stamped or printed on them. The total number made probably ran into millions over the years, yet some collectors will pay a great deal for unusual early-marked specimens which were originally sold for a few pence.

The introduction of the cheap postal service coupled with the invention of the steel pen had greatly increased ink-bottle sales by the second half of the nineteenth century, but it was the government's bill for compulsory education for all children that probably had the most significant and far-reaching effects. When the Reform Act of 1867 added 1 million illiterate and semi-illiterate voters to the list, people in strategic places began to voice concern for the nation's future. Robert Lowe, a former vice-president of the Education Board, speaking on 'Education and the Franchise' commented as follows:

> From the moment you entrust the masses with power, their education becomes an imperative necessity . . . You have placed the government of this country in the hands of the masses and you must therefore give them education.

The removal of 'taxes on knowledge', which included duty on newspapers and paper, greatly encouraged printing and thus increased the desire to learn to read.

Owing to the demand for cheap labour, the actual state of Victorian children in many parts of the realm was deplorable, so it was with some relief that W. E. Forster carried the Elementary Education Act of 1870 for the Liberals. In his speech introducing the Education Bill on 17 February, Forster justified the State taking a much greater part in peoples' education when he said:

> We must not delay. Upon the speedy provision of elementary education depends our industrial prosperity. It is no use trying to give technical teaching to our artisans without elementary education . . . if we leave our workfolk any longer unskilled, notwithstanding their strong sinews and determined energy, they will become over-matched in the competition of the world. Upon this speedy provision depends also, I fully believe, the good, the safe working of our constitutional system . . . I am one of those who would not wait until the people were educated before I would trust them with political power . . . but now that we have given them political power we must not wait any longer to give them education . . .

The effect on literacy in England with the coming of State schools was staggering. Within two decades, the number of men unable to sign their names on the marriage register had fallen from one in twenty to one in five, the ability to read and write increasing at a similar rate among women. This growth in literacy was reflected in an increased demand for newspapers, it being widely accepted that the provincial press developed mainly between 1870 and 1890. Advertising con-

Victorian gum or mucilage bottles, tallest 8¼cm (*Author's collection*)

sequently flourished, and now a not so gullible public was introduced to bottled delights as never before.

Glass was employed extensively for the sale of smaller quantities of ink, bottles of this type being by far the cheapest to produce in the quantities demanded. In order to retail inks for domestic use at approximately one penny per bottle, it became imperative to package the commodity in the cheapest possible way. This involved glassworks in making batches of 1 million containers at a time. They were manufactured in two-piece moulds, and to keep the costs low few were embossed. Cork closures were also used, being driven hard into the sheared lips of these early inks to prevent seepage.

Glass and stoneware ink bottles are plentiful in Britain's late Victorian dumps, the glass containers ranging in colour from aquamarine, light and dark green, through light blue, cobalt and amethyst to varying shades of amber. Stoneware ink pots, in the main, range from pale conicals to dark brown salt-glazed dwarfs, with perhaps a greater colour variation in the master or bulk containers.

Eight-sided aquas would appear to be the most common of Victorian glass ink containers, these mould-blown octagonals having sheared lips and occasionally a base mark. Square and rectangular aquas, usually with vertical ribbing on three sides and pen-rest shoulders, are also quite common, as are the aqua boat rectangulars. Some square bottles in clear glass, often with wider necks, are known to have been used to contain gum or mucilage (a viscous substance obtained from the seeds, bark or roots of various plants), these too being found in considerable quantities by dump diggers.

Because of their small size, ink bottles proved to be of little real value

99

Assorted late nineteenth-century glass inks. Cottage ink on right, 5cm (Author's collection)

as receptacles for other liquids when empty. Frequently they became permanently stained by their contents and were thus discarded in their thousands by rich and poor alike. Less common, however, are the aqua bells and neck-ringed cylindricals. Cottage ink pots with embossed windows and door and occasionally the registration date are considered rare in Britain as are igloos, barrels, tippers, tea-kettles, triangulars, cones and umbrellas. Cobalt, dark green and amber examples are also extremely scarce in any shape or size, British dumps yielding very few indeed.

Some ink containers were designed to be used as inkwells in schools and offices, and their widespread utilization during the final quarter of the nineteenth century was not challenged until fountain-pens by Lewis Edson Waterman and George Safford Parker became established around 1900. The fountain-pen was introduced unsuccessfully in England as early as 1835, but it was another fifty years before Waterman patented the design which was to become the basis of modern fountain-pen development. It was in 1888 that Parker, a young American teacher, made his first pen. Within six years he had patented a device which drained the ink back into the barrel when the pen was upright in the pocket. Parker realized that body heat caused the air in the barrel to expand, allowing ink to ooze into the cap. His modification to prevent this seepage proved highly successful and became known as Parker's 'Lucky Curve' due to its shape.

If ink bottles have improved from the early mould-blown, sheared-lipped, tear-impregnated aquas with their cork and wax closures, then so too have the writing fluids they contained. Prior to the discovery of synthetic dyes by Hofmann and Perkin in the second half of the nineteenth century, fluid inks were usually suspensions of pigments and natural dyes in a weak solution of gum. Initially it was found that the crushing and maceration of gall nuts (the finest being the Blue Aleppo

Gall from that ancient Syrian city) produced the gallic and tannic acids needed to make ink. These acids, together with a solution of copperas, were made into a straw-coloured concoction in hot water, which slowly turned black when exposed to the air. This black ink was much cheaper to make than coloured inks, but unfortunately formed a black deposit in the bottles. The addition of sulphuric and hydrochloric acids was found not only to prevent this corrosion from taking place, but also to keep the fluid clear.

Of the early coloured inks, Victorian price lists show greens, blues and carmines as the most expensive. Verdigris produced green, whilst a stable salt-free colloidal solution was required for blue. The crimson-red of carmine was brought about by dissolving cochineal or diluted acetic acid in ammonia, but bottles containing this ink had to be fitted with stoppers of ground glass to prevent rapid evaporation. As many of these coloured inks were aimed at a feminine market, manufacturers were quick to appreciate the potential for perfumed varieties, 'scented writing fluids for ladies' being very much in vogue from mid-Victorian through to Edwardian times. An advertisement from the 1860s, whilst not yet exploiting perfumed ink, came fairly close:

Glover's Encre à la Violette. The Lady's Writing Ink. The beautiful preparation, from its exquisite colour resembling the flower whose name it bears, is the most elegant and unique appendage to the fashionable writing-desk.

This particular brand of violet writing fluid was sold in 6d (2½p) and 1s (5p) bottles of light blue glass, and is indicative of the part played by colour (and later by scent) in attempting to capture a specific feminine market for the ink industry.

August Hofmann, a German chemist working in London, discovered how to obtain aniline from coal-products, so that the aniline known as 'Hofmann's Violet' was used in the making of ink from 1863. Eosin, a red dye produced by the action of bromide on fluorescein, was discovered by Caro in 1874, yet it was a British research chemist by the name of William Perkin who made the discovery of mauve from coal-tar as early as 1856. Therefore, it was really this early piece of detection which led to the foundation of the aniline dye industry. Coloured inks made from coal-tar dyes, such as methyl blue, methyl violet, magenta, etc., were particularly fugitive in conditions of light or damp, however, and were eventually replaced by more suitable synthetic dyes.

Considering the cheapness of their manufacture, it is somewhat surprising that so many glass inks have survived intact the rigours of Victorian waste disposal. In point of fact, they often possess numerous tears (trapped air bubbles) in their structure indicating inferior bottle-making techniques or the use of poor quality batch ingredients. As previously mentioned, few English glass ink bottles were embossed between 1850 and 1900, although a small number of late-Victorian bottles do carry the embossed name of the ink manufacturer. A good example of this is the famous London ink firm of H. C. Stephens, whose aqua bells incorporate the name of the company on their base. Angus & Co had their name embossed on the base of rectangular aquas, whilst others had brand names or symbols, such as 'Queen Sheba Gold' (gold ink) or a lion, embossed on one side panel. Inks imported from the United States during the last two decades of the nineteenth century, have the appearance of being more robust than their British counter-parts. Usually in clear or aqua glass and with hand-worked neck finishes, American glass inks found in Victorian dumps include those of Haley (a clear or aqua cylindrical embossed HALEY MADE IN USA INK CO); Parker (a square ink in clear glass embossed THE PARKER PEN CO JANESVILLE WIS on the base); Davids (another clear square with base embossment THAD. DAVIDS CO NY); Carter (a clear cylindrical with side embossment CARTER'S INK and a base embossment MADE IN USA).

Some English pen and ink manufacturers, such as L. E. Waterman & Co, had perceptively established themselves in North America by the turn of the century, whilst American companies, such as Parker, Thaddeus Davids, and the New York firm of Mabie, Todd & Bard, had reversed the procedure. Thaddeus Davids, for example, had registered a design patent in England for a white stoneware bulk ink pot complete with pouring lip as early as 1858, its incised registry mark incorporating the date of 3 November.

Mabie, Todd & Bard were operating from at least four addresses simultaneously in the England of 1893. Their 'Swan' fountain pen was marketed in three sizes at 10s 6d (52½p), 16s 6d (82½p), and 25s (£1.25), with a choice of nibs ranging from 4s (20p) to 11s (55p). The pens were apparently acknowledged as being 'as perfect as inventive skill will admit'. Advertising from its Oxford Street base in London in the autumn of 1899 another American firm, the Parker Pen Co, claimed their jointless 'Lucky Curve' fountain pen to be the greatest improvement ever made in fountain pen construction. The instrument was not only supplied with the very finest fourteen-carat gold nibs, but also had: 'No screw to break. No old-fashioned nozzle. No joints to leak. Perfection.'

American and English stoneware ink pots found in Victorian dumps and bearing registration or other impressed pottery marks are reason-ably forthcoming, some collectors specialising in very fine and

(*Left to right*) 'Unspillable' glass inkwell, 4½cm, late nineteenth-century Haley (USA) ink bottle, 7½cm including cork, pewter-topped paperweight inkwell, 6½cm (*Author's collection*)

Early nineteenth-century stoneware inkwell (*Line drawing by Norman Stockton*)

A Victorian pottery at Longton, Stoke-on-Trent (*Author's collection*)

aesthetically appealing bottles from this group. A particularly fine specimen inkwell in this range came in the shape of an open-mouthed human head, and was probably introduced prior to Victoria's accession. The head was tilted back to allow for the retention of writing fluid within the mouth, and also for a vertical pen rest in the form of a circular aperture in the middle of the forehead. In salt-glazed brown stoneware, the gargoyle-type inkwell is somewhat unusual and highly sought after by collectors of pottery inks. It was possibly first manufactured and marketed by Bourne of Denby in the 1830s when the great bulk of stoneware pieces produced by the firm were of the salt-glazed type and fired in Joseph's new and improved kilns.

Stoneware bulk ink pots were made in considerable quantities in England and France in the latter part of the nineteenth century, but the Americans preferred glass, and emulated only the design. Some master inks in cobalt blue glass and embossed with the names of well-known ink companies like Thaddeus Davids of New York, Blackwood & Co of London, Hyde's, etc., have been found in Victorian dumps, but not in anything like the same quantities as their stoneware counterparts.

Denby Pottery produced thousands of vitreous stone ink bottles

Dwarf and conical stoneware inks, tallest 9cm (*Author's collection*)

Price, Bourne and Stephens stoneware master inks with pourers, tallest 26½cm (*Author's collection*)

105

throughout Victoria's reign, and sometimes included customer's names in their incised marks. The London ink manufacturers, P. & J. Arnold, were one such example, being fairly common to dump diggers. This firm also used small conical stoneware ink wells at their Aldersgate Street Works for their 'Superior Writing Fluid'. These light brown containers were not usually marked, but carried a gummed label and had a cork closure. Stephens issued a similar cone in light grey stoneware for marketing their 'Superior Black Fluid Ink'.

The containers manufactured by Price, Bourne, Lovatt & Lovatt, Angus & Co, P. & J. Arnold, Stephens, Port Dundas (also makers of fine whisky jugs), Carters, Stiff & Sons, are among the better known bulk stoneware inks so far recovered from the refuse tips of Victorian Britain. Most are cylindrical, with pouring lips, and have either the potter's or the ink manufacturer's name (or both) incised near their base. Most of them originally carried some form of labelling. Master inks with a difference, however, were those made by Doulton of Lambeth, for although cylindrical, they had unorthodox shoulders surmounted by a squared neck. Lipped on one side, this neck was secured by a slender elongated cork which was possibly waxed above the lip. These light brown containers not only bore the firm's name and class mark (eg 21 DOULTON LAMBETH), but also the diamond-shaped registration mark of the British Patent Office. This mark facilitated the dating of containers from 1842 to the end of the Victorian era.

Clear glass inkwells with funnel-type openings are also quite popular with collectors, and were reasonably common during the late nineteenth century. Because their contents were not easily spilled when overturned, these funnel wells soon found their way into hotels and offices throughout the world. Their one flaw, perhaps, lay in the difficulty of cleaning them, but this was overcome in later versions by having a hole in the inkwell's base. This was then secured with a rubber plug or metal screw.

Some fine paperweight inkwells were made between 1850 and 1900 in both England and the United States, many originating from the famous Stourbridge Glassworks in Worcestershire. Usually in thick-based clear glass with hinged pewter lids, they are found in attics, cellars or lumber-rooms of old Victorian and Edwardian buildings. They do occasionally crop up in late nineteenth-century dumps, although eighty years of corrosion have done little to enhance their metal closures. Both the funnel and paperweight Victorian inkwells, incidentally, make attractive pen holders for the modern study desk, especially when combined with the streamlined writing instruments of today.

7
POT LIDS

Probably the major disadvantage facing early Victorian vendors of commodities such as bear's grease, fish paste and potted meat was that their goods lacked visual appeal. The answer, of course, lay in the development and introduction of pottery food containers with full-colour underglaze transfer-printed lids. These beautifully executed receptacles appealed to the Victorian eye, and in so doing popularized the preparations they contained.

George Baxter, the Sussex engraver and print-maker, had developed and patented a special process for printing in oil colours as early as 1835. Using a copper plate for his outlines, with neutral tones on the same plate obtained by aquatint, his process required a combination of between ten and twenty wood and metal blocks for each production. Baxter applied his method successfully to Victorian book illustrations and prints, which sold in their hundreds to delighted Londoners and provincial collectors alike.

The main pottery manufacturers concerned with developing techniques similar to Baxter's during the 1840s and 1850s for use on pot lids were F. & R. Pratt & Co of Fenton, John Ridgway, Bates & Co of Hanley, and T., J. & J. Mayer of Burslem. Of these three, the most prolific output was that of Pratt's who had the artist-engraver Jesse Austin in their employ. Austin's method was to engrave a series of inter-related colour plates in copper from which thousands of impressions could be transferred to ceramic lids. The key plate or whole design (on early lids printed in black, but later in brown) was engraved in line and stipple, whilst the other colours (yellow, blue, green, pink) were engraved in stipple only. The impressions were taken in the same way as for ordinary copper plate printing, a finely surfaced strong yet absorbent potter's tissue having been perfected by the Staffordshire firm of Fourdriner in the 1840s.

A leather boss was used to apply the ink, and the engraved plate was then wiped clean. The ink remaining in the lines and stippling would thus form an impression on dampened potter's tissue capable of being transferred directly on to the bisque pot lid. The tissue was subsequently removed in water, and the ink allowed to dry for twenty-four hours prior to the next colour application. It was also necessary for each colour to be in perfect register. Usually this was achieved by incorporating tiny circles in the engravings as part of the pattern. Equidistantly situated in or near the border design, they can be seen quite clearly in the fired transfer of such Pratt polychromed lids as 'The Lovers', 'The Peasant Boys', 'The Bear Pit', 'Alas! Poor Bruin', or 'The Queen, God Bless Her'.

When printing was completed, the colours were fixed to the ware and the oils removed by firing. The lids were then dipped and packed carefully on their rims in saggars prior to being placed in glost kilns for glazing. Made of refractory clay, the large saggars served the purpose of preventing the glaze on the lids from becoming stained by smoke and fumes. First the bottom of the saggar would be covered with lids, then stilts and a tray (also made of refractory clay) added, plus another layer of lids and so on. Sometimes manufacturers would use special kiln furniture in the form of iron tripods or small clay thimbles to prevent glazed ware from fusing to saggars and trays. Others, however, preferred to wipe the lid rims clean of glaze after dipping and thus precluded adhesion in this way.

Although this process of polychrome underglaze transfer-printing only had a relatively short existence, an amazingly wide range of pattern subjects were introduced to pot lids within this forty year period. During the second half of the nineteenth century the Staffordshire potteries of T., J. & J. Mayer and Bates, Elliot & Co of Longport, F. & R. Pratt & Co of Fenton, John Ridgway, Bates & Co and their successors of Cauldon Place, and H. G. & D. Kirkham of Stoke produced lids depicting animals, birds, country and interior scenes, buildings, military subjects, portraits of the famous, Shakespearean landmarks, trade exhibitions, children, sport and other sundry human and inanimate material.

Possibly the most interesting facet of the polychrome process is the way in which it was first used to illustrate the products contained in the transfer-decorated jars. Pratt's, for example, produced a number of containers for bear's grease, the lids of which depicted this unfortunate animal in various humiliating postures. Suitably perfumed bear's grease and other fats were sold to fashion-conscious Victorian males as a form of brilliantine for the hair, and were imported mainly from Russia and Canada after 1850. The Burslem pottery of T., J. & J. Mayer, on the other hand, are known to have been producing shrimp paste pots for the Ramsgate firm of Tatnell & Son in the 1850s. Scenes

Bear's Grease pot, c 1828 (*Courtesy Yardley & Company Limited*)

included lobster and shrimp fishing in Pegwell Bay, and views of the Kentish castles of Sandown and Walmer further south. The firm also dealt with the Cauldon Place Pottery of Shelton and with F. & R. Pratt & Co, but this was not until the mid 1860s and 1870s respectively when Tatnell's had been bought out by Samuel Banger, whose name can be seen on later editions of the 'Belle Vue Tavern' pot lid which contained his fish paste.

Although some lid designs were obviously limiting to their pot's contents, many were deliberately chosen to 'sell' a much wider commodity range. Lids depicting Queen Victoria, St Paul's Cathedral, Crystal Palace, Windsor Castle, Wellington, the Houses of Parliament, Buckingham Palace, Crimean War, Grace Before Meals, etc. were admirably suitable packaging for products ranging from anchovy and chocolate pastes to pomades and relishes, due to their topicality.

Jesse Austin's 'Grace Before Meals', incidentally, is reputed to be the first viably commercial full-colour transfer-printed pot lid to go into production. Austin used five plates for this picture, beginning with blue, then yellow, brown and red. The key plate for this early polychrome lid was printed in black, indicative of Austin's initial full-colour experiments at Lane Delph, for his later key plates were printed in brown. Indeed his later research revealed that brown when superimposed on blue produced a beautifully impressionable sable, totally lacking the variance caused by the singular application of a black ink. It is worth bearing in mind, that the young Austin would have first become familiar with the crude form of multi-colour printing when he first worked for the pottery of William Davenport & Co in the 1820s, and that by the time he moved to Pratt's in 1846 he had become without doubt one of the finest artist-engravers in the industry at that time.

The firm of F. & R. Pratt & Co dates back to the 1770s when William Pratt, a master potter, established a pottery at Lane Delph, Fenton. His sons, Felix and Richard, took over the firm from their widowed mother, Ellen, in 1815, their father having died in 1799, and traded under the name of F. & R. Pratt. The business then passed to Felix's sons, Felix Edwards and Thomas, when it became known as F. & R. Pratt & Co, and it was this third generation of master potters who were responsible for pioneering (with Austin) the polychromed lids under discussion.

Apart from the fact that the younger brother, Thomas, was works manager of F. & R. Pratt & Co and thus ran the actual production side of the firm, he remains a somewhat enigmatic figure to date. By contrast, however, Felix Edwards Pratt appears to have been pragmatistic by nature and very much the entrepreneur of the business. Introduced to ceramics at the age of fifteen, it was Felix who was later to form that important relationship with Jesse Austin which made the firm pre-eminent in polychrome underglaze transfer-printing in mid-Victorian England.

By the time Felix had patented his improved design for pot lids in 1848, moulds and dies had been in general use for at least three years, and the Lane Delph Works set the trend in producing four-inch diameter pot lids which were slightly domed in shape. These colour-printed lids were much larger than their later black and white rivals, for craftsmen like Austin required the additional space in order to justify their carefully chosen engravings.

With customers like Cadbury Brothers, J. S. Fry and John Burgess & Son on his books, Felix was the first to acknowledge the invaluable contribution his resident designer-engraver made to the firm's growing success. Austin, of course, was his own chemist and colour-maker and Pratt would have found it impossible to duplicate his formula and methods in the event of his leaving (as he did for a brief period in 1859). Thus, when polychromed lids reached their popularity peak in the 1860s, Austin was commanding a salary which placed him on equal social terms with his employers.

One of the pot lids which Austin probably designed for the Bristol firm of J. S. Fry & Sons, and was used by them in the 1850s, was entitled 'Napirima, Trinidad'. A very beautiful picture in soft colours, the lid depicts a ship in a Trinidad harbour and refers to 'Superior Chocolate Paste'. Due to its rather unusual edible paste content, it is almost certain that the container would have been specially commissioned by Fry's. The firm dates back to 1728 and claims to be the oldest chocolate manufacturer in Britain, and possibly in the world. Because Trinidad was ceded to Britain in 1802, it was perhaps an obvious choice of source for the firm's importations of cocoa, and hence the 'West Indian' lid.

Although the firm was founded by Walter Churchman, it was a young Quaker apothecary by the name of Joseph Fry, trained in the medical properties of plants and herbs and the compounding of drugs, who first realised the great potential of wholesale chocolate making. Eighteenth-century medical literature enthusiastically recommended chocolate as a therapeutic beverage, but eating-chocolate was virtually unknown at this stage. The chocolate being produced by Fry in 1780 consisted, therefore, of soluble tablets to which the consumer added milk or water.

Joseph's son, Joseph Storrs Fry, patented a new technique for grinding cocoa beans in 1795 but, like his father before him, he was an innovator rather than an inventor. To provide the necessary power for his cocoa-grinding apparatus, J. S. Fry had a Watts steam engine installed in his factory. An article in the *Bury and Norwich Post* of 6 June 1798 commented:

> Since the great improvement of the steam-engine it is astonishing to what a variety of manufactures this useful machine has been applied; yet it does not a little excite our surprise that one is used for the trifling object of grinding chocolate – it is, however, a fact, or at least we are credibly informed that Mr Fry, of Bristol, the maker of the famous Churchman's chocolate, has in his new manufactury one of these engines for the sole purpose of manufacturing chocolate and cocoa. Either the consumption of this little article must far exceed our ideas, or, which we think much more likely, a very large proportion of what is drunk in the kingdom must be made by him.

The business eventually passed to Joseph Storrs Fry's three sons, and expanded rapidly from the 1860s onwards. Fry's 'Superior Chocolate Paste' was much in evidence, and the now famous Fry's 'Chocolate Cream' bar was introduced in 1886. The last forty years of Victoria's reign saw the opening of six more factories in Bristol to cope with the firm's increased trade. The company merged their financial interests with Cadbury Brothers Ltd in 1918, becoming a wholly-owned subsidiary of Cadbury's in 1935. The Cadbury Group of companies, which by now included the sweet manufacturing firms of Pascall and Murray, became Cadbury Schweppes Ltd in 1969 following a merger of the Cadbury Group Ltd and Schweppes Ltd. The firm of Schweppes dates from 1792, and is discussed in more detail in the following chapter on mineral waters.

(*Left to right*) Boot's Cash Chemists pot lid, Jewsbury & Brown toothpaste pot, Wood's 'Areca Nut Toothpaste' pot (*Author's collection*)

Attractive as the polychrome lids of Austin and his contemporary artist-engravers in the Potteries were, however, they proved expensive 'wrappings' for pastes and creams, and although many were works of art in their own right, it was inevitable that they be replaced by something less extravagant. Cardboard, tin and glass containers could be manufactured at a fraction of the cost, and the turn of the century saw the virtual demise of coloured lids for commercial use.

This particular market was not entirely lost to cheaper methods, however, for many Victorian ointments, pomatums, creams and pastes were greasy and did not readily lend themselves to the new trends for cardboard and tin. Even where glass jars were employed, it was found that the accompanying paper labels and cardboard lids quickly became discoloured and unattractive, so that ceramic packaging prevailed.

The obvious advantages of underglaze transfer-printed advertising in black on white monochrome does not appear to have been fully appreciated or accepted much before the 1880s when large stores such as Harrods, Fortnum & Mason's, Lazenby's and Home & Colonial made them fashionable. Together with the growth of large manufacturing and wholesale chemists, such as Boot's Cash Chemists of Nottingham, these companies began to place bulk orders for lids bearing their own 'burnt-in' brand names.

One of the most common pot lids found in nineteenth century refuse dumps, both in Britain and North America, contained Jewsbury & Brown's 'Oriental Toothpaste', the export versions having the word 'England' included in the address. This firm began when two young druggists, Jewsbury and Whitlow, opened a chemist's shop in Manchester's Market Street in 1826 and announced the sale of 'the most excellent drugs and perfumery'. Whitlow left the business in the mid 1830s, and within ten years Henry Jewsbury had taken his apprentice and assistant, W. Scott Brown, into partnership. The firm's production of artificial mineral waters (examined more fully in Chapter 8) saw rapid development under Brown, so that when he died in 1891 trade had become so great that new premises had to be erected in Ardwick Green. By this time the firm's 'Oriental Toothpaste' department formed only part of a much larger concern, which was then listed as 'Pharmaceutical and dispensing and mineral water manufacturers'. The firm continued into the twentieth century, when it too was eventually taken over by the giant Cadbury-Schweppes Group in the late 1960s.

Toothpastes, needless to say, were by far the most sought-after commodity to be purchased in pots with black on white advertising lids, for hundreds of small high street chemists up and down the country still insisted (in spite of pressures from the wholesalers) on making their own special brands of toothpaste. Hygiene-conscious Victorians were no longer content with tooth-picks or a piece of rag on a stick with which to rub in salt, soot, soap or whatever else had been recommended. A wide range of natural-fibred tooth-brushes in a variety of shapes and sizes and with handles of bone and wood had flooded the market by the 1890s. One patent was even for a beautifully-made tooth-brush with a replaceable circular head, and boxes containing twelve 'oriental fibre' refills could be bought for 1s (5p).

By the 1880s, the majority of chemists were offering their own or manufacturing wholesalers' brands of areca nut or cherry toothpaste, the former being the most popular. The areca palm was a tree native to tropical Asia, and had seeds known as areca nuts which had purgative properties. The species, *Areca catechue*, yielded the betel-nut which was also featured on advertising lids and was later used in chewing-gum. The cherry toothpaste, which was almost as popular, was merely a coloured variation of the areca-nut paste. Carmine, a crimson pigment made from cochineal, was simply added to the preparation without giving it a cherry flavour.

A somewhat unusual additive to toothpaste was that of wintergreen. From the aromatic leaves of this North American shrub, oil of wintergreen was extracted and used in treating rheumatism and for flavouring. The London firm of S. Maw, Son & Sons manufactured this wintergreen-flavoured toothpaste at its Aldersgate Street Works in the 1890s along with cherry, white carbolic, areca nut and white rose varieties, the latter being marketed in a rectangular container with rounded shoulders.

Often the lids of these rectangular and square-shaped pots were tied on with string, but a paper band usually with the retailer's name and address on it, helped to secure the lids of cylindrical containers. The band, normally about three centimetres wide, was wrapped around the body of the pot, including part of the lid, and had to be torn in order that the pot might be opened.

An interesting trend in pot-lid advertising among the makers of toothpastes was that of attempting to blind the customers with science. Out of the 1,000 or so varieties of toothpaste found so far in British dumps, the Victorian consumer was offered these mind-blowing concoctions: 'Rozalium' (probably pink-coloured), 'Sapaceous' (soapy), 'Charcoal', 'Quinine' (a febrifuge and tonic), 'Thymozol' (possibly a corruption of 'thymol', a crystalline phenol or carbolic acid having a pleasant aromatic smell and used as an antiseptic), 'Menthene' (almost certainly the camphor-like substance known as menthol, which was obtained from oil of peppermint, and used as a local anaesthetic for neuralgia), 'Coralite' and 'Coralline' (indicative of a red or pinkish toothpaste), 'Odontine' (ondontology being the scientific study of teeth), 'Salicifrice' ('salici' derived from 'salicin', a bitter crystalline compound obtained from poplar and willow bark and used medicinally, and 'frice' from the word 'fricare', meaning to rub) and 'Terebene' (a mixture of hydrocarbons obtained by the action of sulphuric acid on oil of turpentine and sometimes used as an expectorant). Others, such as 'Sweet Honeysuckle', 'Iris', 'Carnation', 'Oriental', were chosen purely to conjour images of beauty, freshness and mystery, and thus sold quite successfully.

An English provincial chemist who became well known throughout Britain, the Colonies and North America for his toothpaste during the second half of the nineteenth century, was William Woods of Plymouth. Having established the business in 1850, William was soon making his own 'Areca Nut Toothpaste', 'Dandruff Pomade', 'Rosemary Hair Cream' and 'Far Famed Cough Linctus'. The firm, under the name of Woods & Son, is still in existence. An early advertisement for Woods toothpaste in *Smiths Plymouth Almanac* of 1865 stated that the preparation was:

> recommended by dentists as the best and safest means of preserving the teeth, it removes tartar without injuring the enamel, (as by sealing) and instantly checks inflammation of the gums, rendering them perfectly healthy, and a pearly whiteness is imparted to the teeth by its use.

Woods 'Dandruff Pomade' which was 'to be rubbed into the roots of the hair every alternate morning', was sold in 1s (5p) pots in the 1870s, and lids of this particular item are rare. The firm also manufactured a lip salve, which came in a pot with a small decorated lid bearing the letters M.P.S. after Woods name. William first used these initials on his lip salve containers in the mid 1880s, although he had been a Member of the Pharmaceutical Society for a number of years by then. The title is omitted from the lids of Woods Victorian toothpaste, but appears on the firm's later and slightly larger Edwardian versions.

Victorian lip-salves, of course, were the precursors of modern lip-sticks, and sold in very small pots with lids measuring approximately 40mm across. Initially, these 'ointments' were intended to relieve the discomforts of sore lips, the rose-coloured variety eventually being developed cosmetically into stick form in the 1890s. As with miniature bottles, these tiny lip-salve lids are easily overlooked by the dump digger, or even discarded by beginners as not being worth the trouble of taking home. It is certainly true that at the time of writing, these lids do not generally demand a very high price, but as there are about eighty known types from British dumps, some collectors prefer to specialise in this field. Few lids, however, can be claimed as works of art, many having only a single line border and the minimum of lettering. Attractive lip-salve lids are known (S. Maw, Son & Sons marketed one with a Tudor rose design in the 1880s, for example), but such embellish-ments usually precluded any advertising other than the name of the commodity they contained.

An appreciable number of cold cream pot lids, found in late Victorian dumps, carry very elaborate leaf and scroll designs and geometric patterns, but no manufacturer's name. This was due to the fact that by the 1880s the age of the wholesaler had come into being bringing with it a demand for pots and lids of standard design. This, of course, suited the pottery manufacturers who by this time were finding it increasingly difficult to compete with other types of packaging and welcomed large orders for standardised containers. The wholesalers for their part simply distributed these uniform pots to retail chemists throughout the country together with free printed labels bearing the individual chemist's name and address. These paper labels served the double function of advertising and of efficiently sealing the pot lids to their bases.

An off-shoot of the perfumery business, cold creams naturally contained some of the ingredients found in scents – attar of roses, cream of almonds, myrtle, and so on. Such creams were also the forerunners of modern skin foods and incorporated such medications as zinc (an antiseptic astringent), cucumber (used for its soothing properties), glycerine (which maintained moist conditions in cosmetics) and camphor (an aromatic ketone obtained from a species of laurel growing in Japan and China).

Cold Cream pot lid (*Courtesy Yardley & Company Limited*)

Three cold cream lids quite well known to Australian collectors and found occasionally in British dumps from the late 1880s are those from the Melbourne homoeopathic pharmacy of Martin & Pleasance. These creams or cerates (waxy mixtures) were unusual in that they contained botanic ingredients such as arnica, calendula and hamamelis. As homoeopathy is a system of medicine based on the treatment of disease by the administration of simple drugs in small quantities so as to produce symptoms like those of the disease in a healthy person, the use of herbal or botanic sources would appear somewhat incongruous to furthering this end. Arnica, for example, was a tincture prepared from mountain tobacco and used as an application for bruises. Also used for the treatment of sprains and bruises was calendula, a species of marigold from which an oil could be extracted. Hamamelis was better known to the layman as witch-hazel, and had long been used to ease the painful swellings caused by stings, knocks, sunburn, etc. This astringent extract or oil was prepared from the tree's bark and leaves. Although the number of these lids unearthed so far hardly slots them into the 'fairly common' category, it would seem that their contents did enjoy some measure of popularity in spite of what may have appeared to some to have been a questionable source at that time.

It is perhaps debatable when discussing Victorian cerates as to whether they were cold creams or ointments, for many had contents of similar botanical nature. The Exeter chemist, George Stocker, provides a useful illustration of this with his 'Healing Ointment'. Stocker's medication, in common with those of many of his Australian counterparts, was comprised of carbolated eucalyptus, the West Country pharmacist being one of the few English chemists to use oil from the blue gum tree of the southern hemisphere. Carbolate or carbolic acid is the common name for phenol which is obtained from coal-tar and used especially as an antiseptic, whilst the leaves of the eucalyptus produce oil with a strong characteristic odour which can be used for treating respiratory diseases. It is perhaps interesting to note that many of the active ingredients used in Victorian medicines, such as zinc oxide, menthol, camphor, oil of eucalyptus, oil of cedar wood, turpentine oil (an oleoresin or mixture of an essential oil and a resin from the terebinth conifer of Southern Europe), and thymol (an aromatic antiseptic obtained from oil of thyme), are still present in many of the ointments and creams in use today. Ingredients nowadays, of course, have to be clearly listed on the pots and jars which contain them. This was not the case with Victorian manufacturers, however, and although one or two ingredients were sometimes declared in the title (eg 'Carbolic Ointment', 'Thymolodyne Jelly', 'Marshmallow Ointment'), there was no guarantee of their actual presence.

Professor O. P. Brown's 'Herbal Ointment' pots indicated that they contained the 'great external remedy for rheumatism' together with cures for numerous other ailments such as ulcers, piles, abscesses, tumours and sores. Such advertising claims often proved erroneous, for many cure-alls (like Brown's 'Blood Purifier') were later discredited by an Edwardian panel of the British Medical Association as being little more than coloured water or medicinally useless perfumed emulsifiers.

Probably the most publicised vendor of Victorian ointments was Thomas Holloway of London. Already mentioned in the previous chapter on medicines, this self-styled 'Professor' made his fortune with the aid of large-scale advertising in newspapers and on hoardings and public transport. A typical Holloway advertisement from the late nineteenth century read:

Holloway's Ointment

Assures against Aches and Pains, Rheumatism, Sciatica, Lumbago, Stiffness of the Limbs and Joints, Sprains and Strains. It cures Bad Legs, Old Wounds and Sores with amazing rapidity, and is magical in the treatment of all Skin affections. In cases of Asthma, Bronchitis, Sore Throat, Hoarseness and Tightness of the Chest it gives immediate and lasting relief
Thomas Holloway, 113 Southwark Street, London.

A similar advert for Holloway's 'Pills' ensured that these two 'safe recommendations' could, between them, cure practically every ailment known to man for as little as 2s 9d (14p). Early Holloway pots and lids from his address at 244 Strand carried a variety of typefaces and elaborate scrollwork, whilst others boasted horizontally printed advertising with a 'Mother and Child' trade mark. Lids bearing this specific design, but with an increased price of 3s (15p), were still on sale in the 1920s.

Few lids for shaving-creams are known from before the 1870s, for side-whiskers, beards and moustaches were still popular. Both Prince Albert and John Brown, Queen Victoria's favourite ghillie, had side-whiskers that almost met under the chin. The great Liberal Prime Minister, Gladstone, also favoured this style, although his Conservative rival, Benjamin Disraeli, was content with a 'goatee' beard. Edward, Prince of Wales, had a 'full-set', although by the 1880s younger men had begun to prefer a more clean-shaven look.

A rare scalloped-edge lid from the late 1850s carries the erroneous portrait of a smooth-shaven Prince Consort, an amusing example of the lengths to which a manufacturer would go in order to sell his product. Its impressive trade name, 'Prince Albert's Ambrosial Shaving Cream', almost matches that of its vendor, Napoleon Price.

Boots, the Nottingham-based cash chemists, was one of the first companies to develop its own retailing outlets selling its own factory-made branded goods. A great number of these, including cold creams, toothpastes, ointments and shaving-creams, were sold in transfer-printed earthenware pots. Containers from the mid 1880s for Boots' 'Crème d'Amande' (shaving-cream perfumed with almonds) incidentally had lids which aptly illustrated their contents as being a comparatively new product in that they included directions:

> Spread a small quantity on the beard and use the Brush, having previously moistened it with hot or cold water.

The Hanley pharmacy of Edmund Jones manufactured a 'Superior Rose Shaving Cream' in the final decade of the nineteenth century which produced 'a lasting, luxuriant and emollient lather'. Situated in the heart of the Potteries, this chemist did not have very far to go for his containers – unless, of course, he purchased them ready filled from a wholesaler similar to the Boot organisation, as was the growing trend with the smaller late-Victorian retailing concerns.

Some shaving-creams were, nevertheless, still prepared by individual hairdressers in much the same way as chemists made up their own oint-ments. Numerous Victorian barbers combined the trades of hair-dressing and perfumery, for often their scented creams were advertised as being a combination of shaving-cream and hand-cream – perhaps a subtle form of insurance in the event of shaving being a short-lived fashion. Almonds, roses and violets were popular scent-giving additives for such creams, whilst glycerine was used as a softening agent. Trade names like 'Ambrosial' (meaning the food of the gods, or indeed any-thing delightful to taste or smell), 'Erasmic' (probably implying easy removal of whiskers) and so on, were again of obvious desirability.

Harrod's 'Bloater Paste' pot lid, Maw's 'Otto of Rose' Cold Cream pot lid, Buszard's 'Bride Cake' pot lid (*Line drawing by Norman Stockton*)

Originally, pomade or pomatum cream was prepared from apple-pulp, the words stemming respectively from the French *pomme* and the Latin *pomum*, and both meaning apple. This application or ointment was similar to bear's grease in the sense that it claimed to be both dressing and rejuvenator for the hair and skin of the head. In the sixteenth century, apple pulp was mixed with goose grease, and rose-water added for scent. The preparation was first used as a face cream, but later to promote the healthy growth of hair. Then, as advertising claims grew in extravagance, the commodity's 'powers' were extended to those of hair restorer, curling cream, dandruff eradicator and so on.

William Woods, the Plymouth chemist already mentioned for his tooth-pastes, was manufacturing 1s (5p) pots of 'Dandruff Pomade' in the 1870s, the contents of which had 'to be rubbed into the roots of the hair every alternate morning'. This would seem to have been the vogue in the last quarter of the nineteenth century, for the primary function of the majority of pomades at this time was as scurf or dandruff medications. Adjectives like 'medicative', 'herbal', 'nutritive', 'sedative', 'restorative' and 'rejuvenative' were common on late Victorian pot lids, and give some indication of the careful choice of words used in the early days of advertising propaganda.

Exotic or unusual-sounding words were also much in evidence, the vast choice range in pomades making use of 'Peruvian Balm', 'Castor Oil Pomade', 'Medicated Balm', 'Sulphur Scurf Pomade', 'Pure Herbal Nutritive Cream', 'Eucalyptal Pomade', 'Quinine Pomade', 'Trotter Oil Pomatum', 'Concentrated Egg Julep', 'Macassar Pomade' (oil said to consist of ingredients obtained from the Indonesian port of Macassar), 'Vegetable Pomade', 'Marrow Pomade' (probably the soft fatty substance from the cavities of bones rather than the edible gourd), and 'Trichogenitor' (trichology being the study of structure, functions and diseases of the hair). Some pomades were sold as hair dyes as well as claiming to be hair restorers, and often contained the light brown oil of walnut. Logwood was also employed for this purpose, although the dark-red dye obtained from this American tree was used mainly in ink.

But if advertising lids were sometimes spurious in the extravagant claims they made regarding ingredients, then the pots themselves could be described as being even less genuine when it came down to actual dimensions. The majority of transfer-printed earthenware pots were designed to make them appear to contain far more than they actually did. Comprised of a heavy pottery base and having a wall some 7mm thick, the relatively small capacity of these pots afforded purchasers very little in terms of actual content. An average 70mm pot weighing 200g, for example, would probably have packaged about forty grammes of the product it advertised.

Deception of one kind or another was widespread in Victorian Britain, especially from the late 1880s when monochrome pot-lids for edible pastes were gaining in popularity. The transfer-printed pots of reputable companies such as Crosse & Blackwell, Burgess's, Fortnum & Mason and Savory & Moore, were often subject to re-use as containers for products of inferior quality. As with literally hundreds of other established commodities, this gave rise to numerous court cases and warning notices in newspapers and journals.

A simple example of a reputable Victorian firm's awareness of fraudulent practice can be observed on the lids of Keddie's 'Anchovy Paste'. As well as having its own trade mark, this Westminster company made certain that its customers knew they were buying 'Real Gorgona Anchovy Paste' as opposed to that manufactured by firms of disrepute who used sprats instead of the small dark-green *Engraulis encrasicholus* so esteemed for their rich pungent flavour.

Bloater and anchovy pastes were in great demand by our Victorian predecessors, the most attractive lids for these commodities coming from the Great Yarmouth firm of Blanchflower & Sons and including 'The Fish Barrel' (Anchovy Paste), 'The Yarmouth Fishing Boat' (Bloater Paste), 'The Farm Yard' (does not state the pot's contents, but probably contained potted beef or ham). The New Bond Street fishmongers, Gilson & Sons, supplied their 'Cream of Bloater' (printed in blue) and 'Cream of Prawns' to the aging Queen Victoria in the 1890s, whilst Fortnum & Mason provided pots of their 'Caviar', 'Potted Beef', 'Potted Game', 'Anchovy Paste' and 'Chicken & Ham', with lids bearing the Queen's coat of arms. The firm also sold their 'Mushroom Savoury' in a very attractive domed-lidded pot printed in

Egg Julep, Glycerine Cream and Carbolic Toothpaste pot lids
(*Line drawing by Norman Stockton*)

brown and depicting fresh young mushrooms ready for gathering.

Burgess's 'Genuine Anchovy Paste' lids are among those most commonly found by diggers of Victorian dumps, due to the commodity's immense success as a pounded fish relish from about 1885. Printed in black on a white ground, the lids carry Victoria's royal coat of arms, the firm's Strand address, and advice that the paste be eaten on toast or biscuits.

Rarer paste lids from the Victorian period include those for potted cod's roe, fluid meat, dandelion cocoa, and bride cake. The latter may well have been a novel way of presenting guests with the customary piece of wedding cake, although confectioners like W. & G. Buszard from London's Oxford Street possibly used pots containing (say) sweet-meats to advertise their most artistic manufactures – i.e. wedding cakes.

8
MINERAL WATERS
AND CLOSURES

By the 1830s there were dozens of well-established mineral water springs liberally sprinkled throughout Western Europe and the United States. They had been developed as health resorts to cater for the ailing rich who flocked to them in their thousands. The springs or wells, a number of which were naturally carbonated, were highly regarded as treatment centres for skin diseases, dyspepsia, gout and rheumatism. Many spas, with their beautiful botanic gardens, crescents, pavilions, terraces and assembly rooms, not only became the haunts of fashionable society for their hydrotherapy but also for their social life and gambling. Altitude, climate or water temperature contributed to the success of these resorts, too, although the healing properties of their springs supposedly stemmed from the varying amounts of calcium, chlorine, iron, magnesium, sodium and sulphur they contained. In order to perfect a cure by 'taking the waters', patients were expected to drink as well as to bathe in these natural watering places. The inevitable bottling of such subterranean cure-alls for commercial sale by local authorities and enterprising businessmen saw the beginnings of what was to become our modern soft drinks industry.

Probably the most popular watering-place in the North America of the nineteenth century was Saratoga Springs in New York State, although all the better-known resorts, with possibly the exception of Bartlett Springs in California, tended to be in the Eastern or Mid-Western States. Blount Springs, Alabama, and Hot Springs, Arkansas, are just two that come to mind, the latter having since been made a national park.

It was the Belgian town of Spa in Liège province that lent its name generically to similar centres elsewhere, for it had been famous for its mineral springs since the fourteenth century. The thermal springs of the French health resort, Vichy, were known to the Romans, whilst the hot sulphurous springs of Aix-les-Bains, just north of Chambery, boasted an extremely healthy climate as a bonus. Karlsbad, the German name for the new Czechoslovakian spa of Karlovy Vary in the

Bohemian Forest, was renowned for its alkaline thermal springs. Marienbad, too, was internationally famous for the waters of its springs, which contained sodium sulphate (Glauber salts), used medicinally as an aperient since the sixteenth century. The Black Forest health resort of Baden-Baden, became one of Germany's most fashionable spas in the nineteenth century, as did Nieder-Seltzers with its effervescent mineral waters after which similar artificial mineral or seltzer-waters were named. A bottling firm from northern Germany which has become well known to collectors in recent years is the Appollinaris Company. Their extensive use of salt-glazed Crutchon bottles in the nineteenth century for natural spring waters resulted in the name 'Appollinaris' being taken as a general term for these tall, cylindrical containers. The two common sizes for these brown, shoulder-handled table water bottles are 230mm and 310mm, although smaller and much rarer sizes are known to exist.

In Britain, the natural hot springs of Bath attracted throngs of high-ranking visitors to the city, its Assembly Rooms being acknowledged as the finest suite of eighteenth-century entertainment rooms in the country. Buxton became famous both as a winter resort and for the healing waters of its lavishly marbled St Anne's Well. Situated some 300m above sea level, the Derbyshire spa and market town is the highest of its size in England. Jesse Boot, the wealthy British drug manufacturer, bought a house there around the turn of the century. He suffered badly from arthritis in his legs and was advised by his doctors that the spa waters, together with more exercise, were an essential form of treatment for his complaint. Boot was obviously a great believer in both natural and artificial mineral waters, for in 1894 he opened his own mineral water plant at a cost of £5,000 to supply his shops which then numbered forty-five in all.

The medicinal waters of Cheltenham, the Gloucestershire spa at the foot of the Cotswolds, were being treated and bottled by a man called Thompson in 1806 and were still being advertised in 1901:

Cheltenham Spa Mineral and Aerated Water Co. Manufacturers of the Cheltenham Natural Mineral Waters in Bottles and Half-bottles. Albion Street, Cheltenham.

Like Cheltenham, the North Yorkshire spa town of Harrogate bottled its waters for sale to the general public, using an elongated form of dumpy embossed with the words 'Bottled at the Royal Pump Room Harrogate'. The Warwickshire health resort of Royal Leamington Spa poses little mystery as to how it came by its rather grand title, but unlike

Bath, where spa treatment was ended in 1976, its Royal Pump Room still offers modern hydrotherapy.

An indication of the scope afforded to a Victorian mineral water manufacturer from the provinces can perhaps be seen in the firm of Kinmond and Co who had their premises in Leamington's Kenilworth Street in the early 1870s. The firm had been established for a quarter of a century by this time, and had first supplied mineral waters to Her Majesty the Queen in 1858, and the Prince of Wales some four years later. Under their unusual trade mark of a man balancing on his hands, the firm's advertised commodities included soda water, Brighton seltzer, potash water, lithia water, lemonade and sherryade and could be obtained from:

> ...all Chemists, Grocers and Wine Merchants, at every Hotel in Leamington, and throughout the kingdom, either in the egg-shaped or Patent French syphon Bottles.

Taking advantage of the extensive facilities now provided by the railways (for most major English cities were linked by 1844 and small railway companies swallowed up by 1870) Kinmond's could ostentatiously announce that in the month of July 1873 they '. . . supplied by Rail throughout England, 451 tons of goods, at a carriage cost of £532 12s (£532.60p).' Evidently business was good, for on 14 March 1874, a statement in the *Chemist and Druggist* read:

> Messrs. KINMOND & CO., manufacturers of the well-known Leamington Aerated Waters, eager to ensure the utmost purity of their products, have invented what they term an *apneumatic* process of preparing the water which they employ. Before charging it they collect it in silver-lined cylinders, and by pneumatic pumps exhaust it of previously contained air or gasses. Manifestly the waters thus manipulated will contain only the carbonic acid gas expressly pumped into them; and it is equally evident that an equal pressure will, by this means, indicate a larger proportion of gas.

This investment of plant also led the *Chemist and Druggists' Advocate* (20 March 1874) to comment that:

> The Apneumatic process of KINMOND & CO. is declared to effectually secure the purity and quality of Aerated Waters; and is considered to be the most important improvement in the manufacture of Aerated Waters within the last thirty years.

The adjective 'apneumatic' was applied to a whole range of Kinmond's mineral waters after this date, although some items such as their sparkling spring water, quinine tonic water, orange champagne, green ginger and aromatic ginger ale were excluded. The firm's aromatic ginger ale became very popular in the 1890s, being advertised extensively.

Up until the middle of the nineteenth century, many ginger beers had an alcoholic content of between ten per cent and twelve per cent proof spirit. Restrictions brought about in Britain by the Excise Act of 1855 demanded that non-excisable beverages be less than two per cent proof spirit, which led manufacturers of ginger beer to dilute their brewed concentrates (ginger, liquorice, hops, cloves, gentian, sugar, caramel, brewer's yeast and citric acid) with carbonated water. Ginger beer differed from ginger ale in that it had a higher gravity and a greater proportion of extractive vegetable matter. Ginger beer was usually cloudy in appearance, and for this reason was most commonly sold in transfer-printed or incised stoneware bottles. Ginger ale, on the other hand, was sparklingly clear by comparison and often contained capsicum (cayenne pepper) extracts which increased the pungency of the beverage. Aqua and black glass bottles were found to be unsuitable for ginger beers and ales due to the penetration of light affecting their contents. Ginger beers also lacked visual appeal, so earthenware bottles proved ideal on both counts with this particular commodity. These transfer-printed ginger beers have become extremely popular with collectors, collections often being formed on a basis of closures (some have wedge or screw stoppers), coloured shoulders and necks, comprehensive transfers, and so on. Underglaze transfers did not come into general use on ginger beers until the 1880s when potters were faced with considerable competition from attractively embossed glassware bottles and eye-catching labelling.

Llandrindod Wells was probably the best known Welsh spa in Victorian times whilst others, like Ruthin in the north of the principality, became household names because they were owned by manufacturers of mineral waters. The Royal Welsh Table Water Works at Ruthin was established in 1825 by the firm of R. Ellis and Son Ltd, and according to Rouw's *Guide to Ruthin* (*c.* 1900) was not only the chief industry of the town, but one of the leading mineral water firms in the country. All Ellis's waters were manufactured from the celebrated Crystal Springs, situated on the firm's premises and claimed to be the 'purest water in the world'. Indeed, if the following somewhat over-indulgent extract from the *Medical Press* of 16 April 1890 can be believed, this claim was forcefully supported (like so many others claiming health-giving properties) by medical practitioners:

Ellis's, of Ruthin, as they are best known in the Mineral Water trade, have been recognised for over half-a-century as aiming at, and succeeding in making the very purest and most palatable 'minerals' which art can

Assorted ginger beers with underglaze transfers, tallest $17\frac{1}{2}$cm (*Author's collection*)

produce, cost being a secondary consideration so long as perfection is attained. We should say from a personal examination of the water on the spot a few days ago, that it appears to be as typically perfect a water as could be found at home or abroad.

This being the case, the firm were obliged to issue the following warning against counterfeiters in Sutton's *Trade Directory for North Wales* 1889–90:

CAUTION – The public are particularly requested to observe that every cork is branded R. Ellis & Son, Ruthin; and every label bears our Registration Trade Mark. None is genuine without.

Ellis's trade mark was the famous Welsh ram which was usually embossed on the base of the firm's round-ended, blob-topped cylindrical mineral water bottles. The branded cork was driven in flush with the neck and secured beneath the 'blob' with wire. Labels, too, bore the name of the firm and its trade mark.

It should, perhaps, be made clear at this point that by the end of the eighteenth century analysing chemists such as Black, Cavendish, William Brownrigg and Joseph Priestley had broken the monopoly held by owners of mineral springs who were bottling and selling the natural mineral waters. Having carefully analysed the constituent elements of such waters, it proved relatively easy to manufacture acceptable substitutes at a much lower cost than the originals. Priestley's research, for example, enabled him to impregnate water with 'fixed-air' or carbonic acid gas by dissolving the gas in water using sulphuric acid and chalk. When the extent of the demand for such preparations became clear, syrups were added to make them more attractive to the palate, and all containers of non-alcoholic mineral waters (natural or artificial) became commonly known as mineral water bottles.

London's Drury Lane was probably the first place in Britain to witness the production of artificial mineral waters on any large scale, for it was here that Jean-Jacob Schweppe opened a factory late in the eighteenth century. Sales at this time were generally made through retail chemists, and because mineral waters such as Schweppe's 'Seltzer Water' and 'Soda Water' were then recognised by law as having medicinal properties, they were subject to a duty of 3d on every bottle. This tax was not removed in Britain until 1833 when medicinal claims were proved deceptive. From then on, sales and production of artificial mineral waters began to soar. Schweppe brought several innovations with him from Switzerland, including his own method of saturating water with gas, but although he initially used earthenware bottles for his products, he quickly found them to be permeable to high gaseous pressures and was forced to discard them. When he turned to glass, Schweppe decided in his wisdom to use 'drunken bottles' with rounded ends. The purpose of these egg-shaped bottles, since they could not be stood upright, was to keep the corks damp so as not to allow an undesired escape of gas.

In view of the fact that Jacob Schweppe returned to Geneva in the February of 1799, the designation of 'Hamilton' given to the ovate bottles used by him for aerated waters from early days is a misnomer. William Hamilton of Dublin was indeed granted Patent No. 3232 in 1809 for '. . . the new mode of preparing Soda and other mineral waters, spirituous, acetous, saccharine and aromatic liqueurs and sundry improvements relative thereto', but his specifications stated that he '. . . generally used the glass or earthenware bottle or jar of a long ovate form . . .'; no drawing accompanied this. Specification to Hamilton's later Patent No. 3819 of 1814, which made no reference to bottles in the text, had accompanying drawings of carbonating and

(*Left*) Hamilton and round-ended blob top mineral water bottles, tallest 19½cm (*Author's collection*)

(*Right*) Copeland and Wilson mineral water bottle in pale amber, depicting famous Portland vase, 24½cm (*Author's collection*)

filling apparatus with an ovate bottle attached. For these reasons, it would appear it had been mistakenly assumed that Hamilton invented the egg-shaped bottle, although the container is known to have been in use many years prior to his patent. The prototype probably dates from about 1780 and is thought to have been designed by Nicolas Paul, one of two engineers in partnership with Schweppe in Geneva in 1790. This Genevan father and son team were experts on water-pumps, and undoubtedly contributed much towards their partner's early experiments with artificially carbonated water.

It is interesting to note that in 1859 the firm founded by Jacob Schweppe took over the Holy Well at Malvern and transported thousands of gallons of spa water from the inland resort some 160 kilometres to London. This was hardly surprising when one considers that only eight years earlier over a million bottles of Schweppe's 'Soda Water' were sold at the Great Exhibition alone during the five months it was open to the public. The lease of land and buildings at Malvern, where there was a spring of water suitable for the manufacture of soda

Assorted blob top, internal screw and dumpy mineral water bottles, 1890, tallest 22cm
(*Author's collection*)

and other aerated waters, was apparently held in the 1850s by the firm
of Lea & Perrins of 'Worcestershire Sauce' fame. A feature in the
Malvern Pictorial Weekly of 1855 certainly suggests this, and states that
the Worcester firm was manufacturing 'Malvern Seltzer Water' there
then.

On 25 June 1855, Lea & Perrins agreed to lease to Schweppe the use
of water from the spring and provide necessary storage accommodation
for a period of nineteen years '. . . subject to the Public Rights and the
Rights of the occupier for the time being of the Bath and Pump Room
upon the premises.' Schweppe renewed the lease in 1874, but allowed
it to lapse in 1894 when other wells were placed at their disposal.

It was not uncommon in the 1890s for manufacturers of aerated
waters in larger British towns to produce up to 10 million bottles of
assorted mineral waters in a year, so the dangers of being cut by flying
glass were fairly high. Excessive heat and fatigue may have accounted
for a small percentage of casualties, but often bottles 'flew' due to great
internal pressure being exerted on glassware of inferior structure. In
many cases, the semi-automatic bottling machines were dutifully
guarded and fenced, but even this failed to eliminate entirely the risk to
operatives. Bottles sometimes exploded after they had been filled and

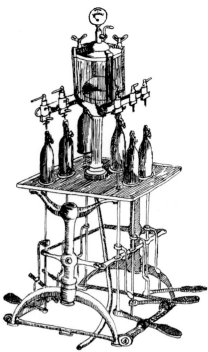

German semi-automatic bottling machine, late nineteenth century
(*Line drawing by Norman Stockton*)

corked; when they were being labelled, crated, stored or loaded, for example. Employees working on the bottling machines increasingly took to wearing gauntlets and face-guards, for the percentage of bottles likely to 'fly' was much greater here than in the concluding stages.

One of the glass mineral water bottles which fell readily into the 'difficult-to-handle' class as far as filling and corking were concerned was, of course, the Hamilton. In response to requests from mineral water firms, however, a flat-bottomed oval had been introduced in the 1870s together with a round-bottomed version. But it was really the 'flat-egg' that had ousted the traditional Hamilton by the end of the nineteenth century, although the latter had been given greater thickness at its neck and shoulders some years earlier to reduce the risk of bursting during filling.

Extracts from an article in *The Mercantile Age* of 15 May 1880 provide further interesting insight into the manufacture of mineral waters by a Victorian company. The establishment in question was the Globe Co of Commercial Road, Glasgow, and the writings examine in some detail bottle-cleaning methods, bottling and syphon-filling processes and export packing:

The various tanks in which the bottles are washed are each in the three divisions; into the first the bottles are steeped in warm water, then passed to the brushes which are rotated by machinery occupying the middle space of the tank, and are finally rinsed by pure water in the third compartment. The rapidity with which the bottles are cleaned is astonishing, and is only equalled by the efficiency of the process. Under any circumstances stoneware bottles are unsatisfactory vessels to clean, as sediment and other impurities cannot be seen, but from the carefulness devoted to cleaning these bottles, and the efficiency of the brushing apparatus to which they are subjected, we are satisfied that no better method can be devised to render them perfectly and thoroughly washed.

In the bottling department, which is a spacious place, we find several machines at work, whose producing capacity amounts to 1,500 dozen bottles per day, filling and corking bottles with great rapidity. The bottles are previously supplied with syrup by means of an ingenious machine which fills the requisite proportion of flavouring extract into the bottles as quickly as they are presented for its reception. This method of syruping the waters vastly supersedes the usual practice of measuring the liquid by spoonfulls, and is cleanly and economical to a degree.

Besides a variety of aerated waters undergoing the process of bottling, we also observe in a side room off the bottling department, ginger beer being filled at the rate of 100 dozen bottles per hour. This is accomplished by a single machine, whose rapidity of action keeps six hands going at an extraordinary rate. The productiveness of this department is very ably assisted by an ingenious patent corking machine, which is capable by extreme pressure of adapting any size of cork to the requirements of every size of bottle; with an aptitude which seems almost human it drops the corks into the bottles as rapidly as they are presented.

The process of syphon filling is prosecuted in an adjoining apartment, and this is accomplished by a machine specially made for the purpose. Syphons have rapidly become popular, from their ready adaptability to the sick chamber, the dinner table, &c., as any small quantity of their contents can be drawn off without deteriorating the remainder. A large trade is done here in these vessels filled with numerous kinds of aerated waters, as is evidenced in the great quantity of syphons we saw undergoing filling. The metallic tops of these vessels are made of an alloy which cannot be affected with the action of carbonated water.

In the packing-room we find many hands engaged filling barrels with the bottled waters carefully stowed with straw, in which condition they are despatched to all parts of the civilized world.

The glassware Hutchinson bottle with its spring wire stopper, which came into being in 1879, was probably the most widely used type of closure for mineral water bottles in the United States until the turn of the century. The vessel was not successful in England, however, although the British patent (No. 1770) was applied for by W. R. Lake on 7 April 1883:

Stoppers; stoppering. – Relates to an internal stopper for bottles containing aerated liquids &c. which is held in place by springs, and to a hook for drawing the stopper to its seat when the bottle has been filled.

Soda water fountains selling a wide variety of popular flavourings could be found in most large towns throughout the States by the 1880s, and it was this market that the Georgian pharmacist and druggist, John S. Pemberton, set out to capture early in 1886. At his home in Atlanta he produced a syrup which was to form the basis of what was to become the best known soft drink in the world, namely 'Coca-Cola'. The trade mark 'Coca-Cola' was first registered in the United States Patent Office on 31 January 1893. At this point in the firm's history the Pemberton family had relinquished all their production rights to the syrup, having sold them to Asa Candler, an Atlanta businessman. Asa's brother, John, was an attorney-at-law and together with Dr Pemberton's partner, Frank Robinson, they formed the Georgia corporation, the Coca-Cola Co. Up until 1894, the drink could only be obtained from soda fountains where it was mixed by the glass on request. In that year, however, the owner of a Mississippi candy company, Joseph Biedenharn, became the first man to bottle 'Coca-Cola', using syrup shipped from Atlanta. Large-scale bottling of the beverage was made possible when in 1899 Benjamin Thomas and Joseph Whitehead secured exclusive rights from the company to bottle and sell 'Coca-Cola' throughout the USA in all but the New England and Mississippi states. The Hutchinson style glass container was used for this purpose until 1902, when it was replaced by the flat-bottomed cylinder purposely constructed to take the crown cork closure. The universally distinctive hobble-skirt shape of today's 'Coca-Cola' bottle was designed for the firm by the Root Glass Co of Terre Haute, Indiana, in 1915, but was not phased into the distribution system until the following year.

Advertising in many of its forms had been well tried and tested by the 1890s, with emergent giants like Coca-Cola quick to exploit the obvious advantages. Yet even relatively small enterprises by comparison were not slow to realise the value of gimmicry when it came to the marketing of goods. Foster Clark Ltd of Maidstone in Kent is a name well known to diggers of Victorian rubbish dumps, the firm's square-shaped fruit juice bottles presenting themselves in considerable quantities. Realising the importance of a good selling name for his products, former grocer's assistant, George Foster Clark, registered the trade name 'Eiffel Tower' in the 1890s, capitalising on the enormous popularity of the iron structure which had been erected in Paris for the Exhibition of 1889. Foster Clark's fruit juice products,

Early Coca-Cola bottles: 1. Hutchinson 1894, 2. Hutchinson 1899–1902, 3. Straight wall 1900–16, 4. Straight wall 1900–16 (*Line drawing by Norman Stockton*)

Jacobs' Pharmacy. First place to sell Coca-Cola
(*Courtesy of the Archives,* The Coca-Cola Company)

(*Left*) First calendar advertising Coca-Cola 1891
(*Courtesy of the Archives, The Coca-Cola Company*)

(*Right*) 1895 ceramic syrup urn (*Courtesy of the Archives, The Coca-Cola Company*)

carrying as they did an embossment of the Champ de Mars modern wonder of the world, sold in their thousands and justified their proprietor's faith in the power of advertising.

There seems little doubt, that the best known Victorian inventor of mineral water bottles was Hiram Codd, who patented his perfected Codd bottle with its odd shape and built-in glass stopper on 3 September 1872. As can be seen from his earlier patents of November 1870 and August 1871, Codd had been experimenting with stoppers and bottlenecks with a view to perfecting his now famous container. The difficulty lay in finding a means of preventing the globular glass closure from returning to the mouth of the bottle whilst the contents were being poured. Hiram Codd's 1872 patent (No. 2621) finally overcame this problem:

> In the neck of a bottle for aerated liquids are formed inclined projecting ridges, one on each side, and the lower part of the neck is contracted. When the ball stopper is pushed in to open the bottle, it rolls down the projecting ridges till it is stopped by the contraction. It is then allowed to roll to the

opposite side of the ridges, which prevent it from returning when the bottle is inclined for pouring the liquid.

Hiram also patented his Codd bottle in the United States of America in 1873, although the design was never very well received there.

Not possessing the business acumen or the capital required to make a financial success of his own bottling company, Codd permitted his 'Original' to be manufactured under licence. One such licencee was Ben Rylands from Barnsley in Yorkshire, who had been running his own Hope Glassworks since 1867. After taking out a licence to manufacture the Codd bottle in 1874, Rylands proved quick to adapt his plant to the successful production of these revolutionary containers. So thorough was the adaptation, that by 1876 Rylands and Codd had combined practice with theory and formed a partnership which was to capture a sizeable slice of the mineral water bottle trade in Britain in the late 1870s.

When Ben Rylands died in 1881, Codd found himself in partnership with Dan Rylands, Ben's son. The younger man was both inventor and manufacturer and had new ideas which he wanted to put into practice. His inventive qualities were initially demonstrated in his patent (No. 1486) of March 1882 which involved improving bottle necks and stoppers. Four months later when a 'Codd, H. – Rylands, D.' patent to facilitate the opening of internally stoppered bottles by means of a neck valve was granted, the partnership seemed to be working. The alliance, however, was doomed to failure. In 1884 Codd, probably resenting the young Rylands' inventive intrusion into what he considered to be his side of the business, returned to his native London after having allowed himself to be bought out by his partner. Codd's inventions to improve bottles and bottling equipment continued until his death in 1887.

The policy of Hope Glassworks was embodied in its trade mark (a figure '4') embossed on all its glassware. This signified four qualities considered by the firm to be of paramount importance with regard to the manufacture of glass bottles – accuracy, cleanliness, neatness and strength. Like his father before him, Dan Rylands firmly believed in the continuation of this policy and thus was able to justify his claim of being the largest supplier of globe-stoppered bottles in the world. At this point (1888) the company was registered as Dan Rylands Ltd, and was marketing at least five best-selling mineral water bottles with marble closures.

The principal feature of the Codd 'Original' was a globe stopper made of glass secured against a rubber washer in the bottle's neck by gas pressure. The 'marble' was prevented from falling into the body of

Patent globe-stoppered variations of the Codd bottle, tallest 19½cm (*Author's collection*)

the vessel (as previously mentioned) by a contraction below the neck, and inclined ridges projected within the bottle held the stopper when the contents were being emptied. The closure was released by means of a pencil-like projection centered in an inverted wooden cup being pressed down upon it, allowing the escape of gas. The Codd 'Empress' had sloping shoulder indentations which facilitated easier cleaning by causing the marble to roll to one side allowing unopposed brush penetration. Codd's 'Reliance' enabled the stopper to be inclined to either side during sterilisation, whilst the 'Acme' of Dan Rylands was similar in construction but included two safety indentations for retaining the glass ball when brushing took place. The 'Crystal Valve' was a glass plunger seated in the shoulder of a bottle which released gas pressure and opened the container when the valve was pressed. This appliance took Dan Rylands a number of years to perfect and is considered by collectors to be the high water mark in the production of internally stoppered glass bottles. The brilliance of its design was unfortunately overshadowed by its cost of production and this, coupled with the lapse of patent protection on Codd's 'Original' bottle, resulted in Rylands being confronted with serious competition for the first time.

(*Top left*) Wood screw chisel stopper, c 1880; (*top right*) Hutchinson spring stopper, c 1879; (*bottom left*) wooden Codd bottle opener; (*bottom right*) crown cork of 1892 (*Line drawing by Norman Stockton*)

When fire caused over £60,000 worth of damage to his Stairfoot Works in 1891, Dan Rylands never recovered. Within two years he was bankrupt, with debts of £200,000, his shares in Dan Rylands Ltd being disposed of, and by 1904 the firm had gone into voluntary liquidation.

The Codd bottle was to become known by a variety of names following its inception in 1872. One such term was 'Alley Bottle' which probably derived from the game of marbles played by children in alley-ways of back-to-back Victorian houses. Codd bottles, with their spherical glass closures, became prime targets for marble-playing youngsters who smashed them to retrieve the 'alleys' they contained. Other appellations included 'Pinch Neck', due to the bottle's constriction above the shoulder; 'Glarney Bottle', of Irish extraction; and 'Marble Bottle'.

Hiram Codd unwittingly provided the science of etymology with a new terminology when beer-drinking Britons used 'Codd's-wallop' to register their disapproval of the carbonated soft drinks contained in the Camberwell inventor's bottles. 'Wallop' was a slang word referring to beer and its potency, and became coupled with Codd's name in the derogatory sense, 'coddswallop' eventually being applied whenever the need for ridicule arose.

So many variations of the original Codd bottle exist that some collections are compiled entirely of these, for apart from those already mentioned, literally dozens of amendments and hybrids were patented between 1872 and 1907. Some of the more familiar adaptations include Dobson's four-way patent, Nuttall's patent, Codd's 'Premier', Foster's 'Niagara', the Skittle, the Bulb, the Round-bottomed, the Fluted base and the Hamilton-Codd Hybrid.

Screw stoppers began to replace internal stoppers in the 1890s although their inventor, Henry Barrett, had first used them in 1872. He patented his idea some seven years later on seeing it used successfully in cylindrical and champagne-shaped glass and stoneware bottles. The wooden or compounded Chisel Stopper with its wedge-shaped head was used in many types of internal screw beer and mineral water bottles in the late 1880s, having been patented by Riley in 1885. The link between Barrett's internal screw stopper and globe-and-plug closures, can be seen in Barrett and Elers containers combining both screw and marble, but these are rare. Internal screw closures gained in popularity after 1900, and are still used in the larger cider bottles of the West Country.

Early bottle closures comprised wads of oiled hemp, beeswax or leather, secured with string. Cork stoppers did not come into general use until the eighteenth century, proving particularly ideal for bottles of the sheared lip variety where the jagged neck of the container could bite securely into the closure and establish a leak-proof seal. Cork is the outer layer of the cork oak, an evergreen tree indigenous to the mountainous regions of Spain and Portugal. Corks had to be cut carefully to ensure that the pores through which the bark of the tree used to 'breathe' were never sliced so that they ran the whole length of them, otherwise the closure would not have been watertight. The manufacture of corks was normally preceded by the preparation of squares which were extracted direct from the board or even from simple pieces, selection often proving difficult and calling for individual assessment. The adhesion of cork to the walls of glass and earthenware bottles was a property which made it possible to ensure the absolute impermeability of the stopper. In addition, as a vegetable product which was completely free from toxic ingredients, the cork stopper did not impart odour, taste or any deterioration to the products it enclosed.

It is perhaps difficult to believe that the swing stopper ('lightning' stopper USA), which was still being used on lemonade bottles in the 1950s, was actually first patented in 1875. It was devised by Charles De Quillfeldt of New York, and commonly took the form of a ceramic plug with an attached rubber washer. The stopper was secured to the rim of the bottle by a hinged wire which could be snapped shut, thus forcing the porcelain plug and rubber washer tightly into the mouth of the container. Slight thumb pressure on either side of the wire bail would loosen the stopper so that it could be moved to one side.

138

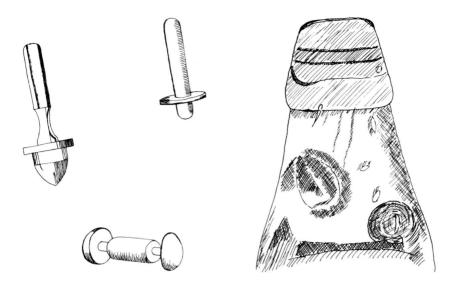

(*Top left*) Long-plug stopper in hardwood; (*top right*) Barrett Elers wooden plug; (*bottom centre*) Bullet stopper (*Line drawing by Norman Stockton*)

(*Far right*) Globe stopper (glass) (*Line drawing by Norman Stockton*)

The arduous and time-consuming practice of having to wire stoneware bottles containing ginger beer had always been undertaken somewhat grudgingly by mineral water manufacturers in the hope that something better would inevitably come along. When the Galtee-More closure was patented in the 1890s, then the mineral water barons might have been forgiven for believing that possibly this was the answer. The traditional stoneware bottle was fitted with a cork held in place by copper wire which passed over the closure and was tied beneath the container's blob top. This also applied to glass mineral water bottles, such as the Hamilton, and was essential to prevent the bottle's gas-pressured contents from blowing out the cork. The Galtee-More Patent was designed in its wisdom to dispense with the use of wire in the accepted sense by replacing it with a single metal pin. A horizontal hole was drilled through the blob top which, the cork having been inserted, could then receive the retaining peg. The cork, needless to say, became tightly wedged beneath the pin thus making it difficult to withdraw. For this reason, and possibly because the closure was patented at much the same time as the crown cork, it aroused very little interest.

Although the glass ball was accepted as being the most widely exploited type of internal closure in bottles used by Britain's soft drinks industry during the last quarter of the nineteenth century, it was certainly not without its rivals. The Hutchinson stopper with its looped wire and rubber gasket has already been mentioned, having been extensively adopted across the Atlantic. Bullet stoppers, too, posed a threat because they could be used in bottles with either body or neck indentations. They were made from glass, porcelain or wood, and included a washer of india-rubber seated either centrally or at one end of a dowel. A localised version sometimes found in the South of England in dumps dating from the 1870s, is the Adams and Barrett internal long-plug stopper. Made from *lignum vitae* ('wood of life') hardwood with a rubber washer at its pointed end and thus having a greater specific gravity than water, the stopper was designed to sink through the liquid (the bottle being filled in an inverted position) into the neck and so close the container as it was removed from the bottling-machine. A similar wooden plug, designed by Henry Barrett in partnership with Charles Elers when the two men formed a small bottling company about 1870, was made under licence in Yorkshire and has come to light in late Victorian dumps throughout the North and Midlands. Guttapercha, a greyish rubber-like substance obtained from juice of various Malayan trees, was often used on early internal stoppers of the bullet and plug varieties. Its one significant drawback, however, was its tendency towards disintegration if left unmoistened for long periods.

The county of Yorkshire seems to have accounted for a great many sizeable glassworks, even when taking into consideration the overall glassmaking standards of Victorian England. Ben and Dan Rylands were, of course, the best known of the Yorkshire glass manufacturers, but other firms such as the Aire & Calder Bottle Works of Castleford, the York Glass Co, Alexander & Co of Leeds and Redfearn Brothers of Barnsley can also lay claim to positions of importance.

The Fishergate Works of the York Glass Co had been established in 1794, and, long before any government regulations relating to graduated measures of flint glass, the company had its own measures specially tested and its own private mark displayed. The term 'York Measures' became known as a measure of the highest quality and accuracy and the company's monogram, a pentagon divided into three parts with the letters Y.G.C. in, can be found on the bases of bottles in most private collections from the Victorian period.

The Old Mill factory of Joshua and Samuel Redfearn had four furnaces in production in the 1860s, with a total of thirty 'working holes'. At that time all bottles were hand-made, so that the working group on each 'hole' consisted of five people: a bottle-maker, a blower, a gatherer, a 'wetter-off' and a 'taker-in'. The last two jobs would have been done by youths who were learning the craft. The earliest existing record of wage rates is dated 1896, when the bottle-maker drew

(*Top left*) Swing stoppered closure showing wire bails and porcelain plug, c 1890; (*top right*) cork and wire closure in blob top neck; (*bottom left*) Thatcher 'Milk protector' (American), c 1890; (*bottom right*) swing stopper, c 1880 (*Line drawing by Norman Stockton*)

£1 13s (£1.65p), the blower £1 9s (£1.45p) and the gatherer £1 5s (£1.25p) for a fifty-two and a half hour week.

According to the trade press of 1887, Alfred Alexander & Co were 'Glass Bottle Manufacturers in Pale Metal'. Their Hunslet Glass Works were the largest in the Leeds area.

The firm's glass works at Blaydon specialised in bottles for pickles, drugs and medicines using amber, green and blue metals, whilst the Southwick manufactury at Sunderland made plain and screw-mouthed bottles in dark glass for wine, ale and beer. One of Alexander's furnaces at Leeds must surely have ranked with the largest in the world, its tank containing some forty-five tons of molten glass. Over 200 employees turned out a thousand gross of bottles every week at the Hunslet Works, whilst the combined factories had their own wharf at Wapping to receive cargoes of bottles from the various works for re-distribution. The group also had their own warehouse at the Great Eastern Railway's Bishopsgate Goods Station.

The final years of Victoria's reign witnessed the beginning of a slow demise in internally stoppered mineral water bottles, for the April of 1891 saw the patenting in America of William Painter's Crown Cork or Crown Cap. This disposable closure of cork-lined crimped metal was intended to close any aerated beverage, had a strong corrugated rim to keep it in place, and did not require to be kept moist.

9
BEER BOTTLES
AND LABELS

The Victorian public house played a dominant role in the social habits of the working classes in nineteenth-century Britain. Until the 1700s beer was brewed at home, a bushel and three-quarters of ground malt and a pound of hops being sufficient to make eighteen gallons of good ale. Publicans, known as brewing victuallers, also brewed beer on their own premises, but the 'common' brewer able to sell beer in bulk had not yet come into his own. The beer trade was profoundly affected in 1830 when an Excise Act introduced beer-house licences which could be obtained merely by paying a fee of two guineas. This meant that any ratepayer able to pay the licence fee could legally sell beer on his own premises without acquiring a Justices' Licence, so that within two months of legislation over 24,000 new retailers were in business.

The Beerhouse Act inevitably brought about the development of a price war between established inns and the newly emergent beer shops in which the adulteration of beer played a major part. It became common practice, for instance, to replace malt and hops with certain cheaply substituted drugs. Watered-down beer was given a delusive strength by the addition of various narcotics, a frequently-used example being *Cocculus indicus*, an acrid Eastern fruit containing the crystalline compound, picrotoxin. This highly poisonous extract when used as a substitute for a due quantity of malt did increase the intoxicating power of beer and porter, but also slowly destroyed the nervous system. Alum, a compound salt pronounced dangerous in 1848 and banned by the first Food and Drugs Act of 1860, turned beer stale if used in too large quantities, whilst the substitution of too many egg-whites (an old ploy to put 'life' back in poor beer) rendered the brew slimy. Quassia, a bitter medicinal tonic taken from the bark and root of a South American tree, was also widely used, as was capsicum and hartshorn. Often a weak brew was tinctured with tobacco and spiced with the romantic-sounding 'Grains of Paradise'. These seeds, which were also known as 'Guinea Grains', came from a tropical West African spice and were a much used narcotic. They contained

Evolution of the beer bottle from eighteenth century to present day (*Line drawing by Norman Stockton*)

Assorted beers. (*Left to right*) 'Black' glass beer with neck holes for swing stopper, embossed beer/mineral water, black glass beer complete with screw top, dark green Bent's beer with lion embossment, tallest 25½cm (*Author's collection*)

opium, and gave liquor a pungent taste when added to it.

Dirty brewing utensils and casks could ruin a potentially good brew quicker than anything, so the utmost care and attention had to be given to cleanliness if profitable results were to be assured. It was essential that the application of soap, or indeed any greasy substance, be avoided and that vessels received meticulous scrubbing and rinsing with boiling water. Bay-salt or stone-lime were sometimes used for cleansing purposes, the utensils being washed afterwards with clean water. Wooden casks which had turned musty or stank of sour beer were treated with alkalised water (lye) and beech ashes. Unslaked stone-lime in boiling water was another useful Victorian remedy, as was powdered charcoal and oil of vitriol (concentrated sulphuric acid). Some coopers even used the method of completely charring the inside of casks over a brisk fire. The barrels were then filled with boiling water, the ebullition being repeated two or three times before they were considered 'sweetened'.

In spite of conscious efforts towards hygiene by some landlords and brewers, dubious conditions still prevailed in many of the less reputable beer-selling establishments, and cried out for a measure of reform. In 1869, it became a legal obligation to obtain a Justices' Licence for the sale of beer and cider, requiring licencees to maintain certain standards regarding habitation and methods of brewing. The Act put many beer shops out of business, but led to a general improvement in amenities.

Inevitably, some small publicans looked for financial help to the brewers who supplied them – great names in the brewing trade like Whitbread, Thrale, Barclay & Perkins, Courage, Reid & Co, Watney, Truman & Co, Bass, Ind Coope, Worthington and Allsopp, each one by then a well established concern. These rich family enterprises were only too pleased to put money into such retailing outlets, ensuring that in return they became tied to the brewery for their supplies. The expansion of the tied-house system throughout England in the second half of the nineteenth century saw the big brewing companies not only advancing capital for structural improvements, but also buying up the properties completely in many cases. Pubs in Ireland, however, remained in the hands of their publicans who were often wine and spirit merchants and whiskey bonders to boot.

The system of payment by truck (paying wages in goods instead of money) was widespread in most industries in the early years of the nineteenth century and did a great deal to foster the beer house in specific areas, for although an Act of Parliament prohibiting it was passed in 1831, the method persisted in some regions as late as the 1870s. Workers were sometimes paid partly in cash and partly in goods which had to be obtained from the company store, the monopoly enforcing unfairly high prices. The butty system, which operated in mining areas throughout the Midlands, was often connected with the truck system. The butty contracted with the mine owner to deliver coal at a fixed price, the contractor hiring his own labour and providing the necessary tools. Usually the contractor was also the owner of a store or a pub, and thus paid his men partly in household commodities, partly in beer, and always at inflated prices. Wages were paid on a Saturday night, and as the public house was the focus for burial clubs, friendly societies and the like, it was also the chosen place for the weekly pay-out. Outside, the wretched mining families would wait helplessly whilst much of what was left of the household's money was drunk away by the husband to the great satisfaction of the publican.

Possibly the first brew to become popular with the working classes on a national basis was the thick, dark, well-fermented bitter beer known as 'porter'. It is thought to have been introduced by a London brewer called Harwood who ran the Blue Last Tavern at Shoreditch in the 1720s, and whose customers were mainly carters and porters from the local markets. Apparently, they were in the habit of requesting brews to be mixed when they ordered a drink, which decided Harwood to develop a beer with the combined merits of his entire range. Charrington, Whitbread and Guinness were just three of many famous brewing names who, helped by a consolidated network of railways which had made possible a national market and in consequence larger business units by the 1850s, built their reputations on this black, top-fermented beer brewed with the finest roasted malt.

A government tax on glass had made the production of bottled beer uneconomic until its total abolition in 1845, but now that the way ahead was clear, this new method of purchase quickly proved welcome. Brewers were forced to cater to public demand by massive re-organisation of fixed capital or at least the buying up of new premises to cope with the expansion. In 1868, for example, Whitbread made the decision that their draught and bottled beer divisions of the business should become separate enterprises. A new building was thus acquired in London's Worship Street (Finsbury) for their bottling stores. Such a public demand for bottled beer was created, however, that these premises were outgrown within a year and the bottling division moved to much larger quarters at Gray's Inn Road. By the 1880s the stores included a washing and rinsing department, a drying gallery, cork and stationery stores, filling, corking and labelling departments, as well as store-rooms and carpenters' shops. The installation of a Loft's patent bottle-washing machine, incidentally, enabled the department to wash and rinse up to thirty gross of bottles per day. Initially the corking department employed hand-corking methods which entailed each bottle being firmly held in a leather 'boot' between the workman's knees. The cork was then driven in with a small wooden hammer known as a 'flogger', a skilled operative being able to cork about 3500 bottles a day. Ebonite screw-stoppers employed by the firm towards the end of the 1880s were, and still are when used, finally tightened by hand. Having anticipated the potential demand and popularity of bottled beers, Whitbread, like many of their competitors, had established a network of production depots throughout the provinces by 1900.

What was to become the largest porter and stout brewery in the world began when Arthur Guinness purchased a small porter brewery at St James's Gate, Dublin, in the latter half of the eighteenth century. The business was confined to the Irish market until the mid 1850s, however, when Benjamin Lee Guinness, son of the founder, decided to establish agencies in Great Britain, Colonial Britain, Europe and the United States of America. The export trade boomed, making Guinness a household name throughout the westernised world. The company became of limited liability in 1886, giving freely to charitable institutions, social welfare and scientific research. The criticisms of Victorian temperance movements were answered by a £150,000 gift to restore Dublin's St Patrick's Cathedral between 1860 and 1865, grants to aid medical research at the Lister and Radium Institutes, and money to finance great slum-clearance schemes in Dublin and London.

It must be noted, nevertheless, that in this golden age of Victorian prosperity the consumption of alcoholic beverages had risen to something like thirty-four gallons per head for every man, woman and child in the country by the mid 1870s, with something like twenty-five per cent of each family's income being spent on drink. Brewers had long since set the example of establishing their premises on corner sites, thus being in a commanding position to attract trade from two or more streets at the same time. Thus few drinkers remained wanting when it came to locating a handy source of supply.

The 1890s saw the continued decline of public taste for porter in much of Britain, although it went on to become the national drink of Ireland. Its popularity was finally replaced by stout in the north as late as the 1970s. With bottled beer fast becoming recognised as a standard drink, various closures were adopted between 1860 and 1900 including corks, swing stoppers and internal screws. Most beer bottles from this period were made of 'black' glass to prevent light penetration from 'turning' the brew. The glass was coloured by adding a quantity

Collection of late nineteenth-century beer labels. (*Courtesy Guinness Museum*)

of iron oxide to the melt, although a true black metal was never produced in this way. When held up to strong light, bottles usually appear a very dark green or brown, according to their metallic content. These containers were almost always prolifically embossed with names of large and small breweries and, where faced with imitations, coupled with slogans like 'Buying selling or using this bottle is illegal'. Embossing also included ornate trade marks which have become the focal point of very fine collections.

Embossing never really took the place of labelling in the nineteenth century, and indeed the two were increasingly designed to complement each other. Numerous permutations of wording, embellishment and illustration were adapted by both glass-maker and printer, although the discovery of lithography by the German engraver, Alois Senefelder, in 1796 made possible whole new horizons for the early Victorian calligraphists in illustration and printed lettering. The outcome was demonstrated succinctly in the monochrome beer cask labels of the 1860s and 1870s. By this time the reproduction of varying shades and colours was no longer a limiting factor and led, through the use of half-tone screens for colour separation, to the possibility of a label being produced in eight or nine different colours. In practice rarely more than four or five colours were ever used on late Victorian beer labels, most brewing companies being content with three. A great many labels bore either the signature or trade mark of the brewery, whilst the two 'new' typographical forms which had been added to the faces of Didot and Bondini, namely Grotesque and Egyptian, were now widely employed. The Burton-on-Trent brewery of Thomas Salt & Co, for example, used the basic form of Grotesque for its East India Pale Ale label. Black wording and embellishment on a green ground were surmounted by the company's trademark of a red Maltese cross in a white circle. The whole was ringed in black on white, and an allowance made for a cartouche to take the name of the retailer, which would have been added at the point of sale. Watney preferred the simpler approach of dark brown on a pale ground for their London Stout label, but still retained their majestically-poised stag trade mark, symbolic of the company's Stag Brewery in Pimlico. Combe & Co, on the other hand, went for a colour combination of royal blue and gold with white lettering for their version of London Stout. The Oswestry brewery of C. Drew employed red and black lettering on a light blue ground for their attractively illustrated Winter Stout label. The brown-shaded label for Allsopp's India Pale Ale had a shaded Grotesque type face, with the company's famous 'upheld hand' trade mark in the centre, its monochromed export counterpart being printed on yellow paper. The watchful eagle of Trueman, Hanbury, Buxton & Co contented itself with a ground of shaded green for its Invalid Stout label, whilst Reid & Co's griffin was emblazoned on a golden ground and enclosed in a white Double Stout ovoid. This fabulous creature with eagle's head and wings and lion's body was afforded a red ground when heralding Reid's Imperial Stout.

Collectors fortunate enough to have labelled beer bottles can learn a great deal from the wealth of information they contain. We know that Lewis & Barker's Wellow Brewery at Grimsby bottled an oatmeal stout which was strongly recommended for invalids. Medical opinion, spurious or otherwise, claimed the recipe of oatmeal, malt and hops from which the stout was brewed to be 'most nourishing and strengthening'. The Eagle Brewery with its raised-winged eagle trade mark claimed that its Davenport-made Double Stout was specially recommended for 'families and invalids', inferring perhaps that it was also beneficial to children. The Dorchester Brewery of Eldridge, Pope & Co attempted to safeguard against forgery by displaying the firm's signature beneath its castellated shield trade mark, as did many of the

Limited edition of 'Hardy's Ale' in Victorian bottle (*Courtesy Eldridge, Pope & Company Limited*)

more reputable companies. The Victorian novelist, Thomas Hardy, enjoyed Eldridge, Pope & Co's full-bodied Single Stout and other brews, for he described 'this beer of Casterbridge' (Dorchester) in glowing terms when he wrote 'The Trumpet Major' in 1879. Much to the envy of Britain's early bottle collecting enthusiasts, the Dorset brewery discovered some 2,000 empty Victorian beers in the 1960s and produced a special unpasteurised and 'limited edition' of Thomas Hardy's Ale in commemoration of the writer's associations with the company.

Bottle devotees will be aware that the famous red triangle representing Bass & Co's Pale Ale was the first trade mark to be registered at the Patent Office's Trade Marks Branch in London's Southampton Buildings where it was certified that:

> ... under date the 31st January 1888, Bass Ratcliff and Gratton, Limited (incorporated on the 18th day of January 1888 under the Companies Acts 1862 to 1886) of Burton on Trent in the County of Stafford, Brewers, are entered on the Register of Trade Marks as proprietors of the Trade Mark No 1 ...

Bass labels were known to have been faked in Britain and France in the 1880s and 1890s, which prompted the company to print on them the following warning:

This label is issued only by Bass & Company Brewers Burton on Trent.

Other well known brewers including Barclay Perkins, Combe, Reid, Whitbread, Eldridge, Pope, George Gale, Jameson and Findlater did the same. Another famous brewery, Worthington & Co, seemed content to protect themselves with the slogan 'Brewers by appointment to H.R.H. the Prince of Wales', the future monarch's emblem, and their own trade mark. Whitbread, however, made no secret as to why they had registered a trade mark for protection. Labels issued by them read:

> Whitbread's celebrated London Stout having suffered severely from forgery of their labels have adopted the above trade mark.

Non-alcoholic brews like Kops Stout and Royal Lager Stout (a contradiction in terms) did not appear to fear from industrial espionage at all, perhaps because the competition was less severe in this field. Muir & Sons incorporated a picture of Calton Hill Brewery on their Sparkling Edinburgh Ale labels, but Bentley's Yorkshire Breweries Ltd decided, rather dourly, to number theirs.

One of the first trade mark labels issued in Ireland by Arthur Guinness Son & Co was to T. & J. Clarke of Capel Street, Dublin, on 16 January 1896. Because the policy of the St James's Gate Brewery was to provide hundreds of retailers like Clarke's, including family grocers and wine and spirit merchants, with bulk supplies of Guinness to be bottled and sometimes blended on their own premises, the firm's 'harp' label was, perhaps, more vulnerable to forgers than most. It is worth remembering here, that photography had been discovered in the 1820s by Joseph Niepce, and that further research with Louis Daguerre saw the perfecting of the 'daguerrotype' process. This involved the obtaining of a photographic image on a copper plate using a light-sensitive layer of silver, iodine and bromide, so that by the end of the century photography could be adapted to photomechanic reproduction methods. It follows, therefore, that offset printing (the transfer of ink from a newly printed surface to another surface so that the final impression is in the same sense as the plate or type) was probably available from the 1880s onwards and could easily have been applied to the forging of labels, especially by French printers who were in advance of everyone else. This, however, in no way precluded a good engraver from copying a label design on to a plate or series of plates capable of reproducing thousands of counterfeits, and this was often the case.

Guinness's labels for stout, be they Extra or Export, were probably the most forged in the British Isles, particularly following the great export drive in the later years of Victoria's reign. Overseas brewers possibly thought themselves out of reach regarding charges of fraud, openly advertising their own brews as Guinness. One trader in Lisbon (whose premises were ironically situated in the Bow Street area of the city) blatantly advertised that 'Corken's Stout is Guinness Stout', and even offered £1,000 reward to anyone who could prove differently. A man typical of a flamboyant age in advertising, John Corken claimed that he was 'not afraid of the analyst or law courts', and then proceeded to state that 'Corken's Rum and Whiskey cures *all* Diseases'.

Imitations must have been going on for some time because in 1868 the Dublin firm of E. & J. Burke, one of the legalised bottlers of Guinness, announced that they planned to introduce their 'New Capsule' (waxed and stamped) as part of the battle against the forgers of labels. A letter giving details read:

Gentlemen,
   The facilities of forging Labels, no matter how carefully they may be made, having lately been very strongly impressed upon us, we have been forced to seek a really perfect safeguard for our bottlings of Messrs. A. GUINNESS SON & CO'S EXTRA FOREIGN STOUT. We are glad to say we have found it, though at a very serious cost.
   After the first of September next, we shall put nothing in bottle, WINES, STOUT, ALE, or SPIRITS, without our 'NEW CAPSULE', having upon the top our Name and Trade Mark in Red Letters on a Yellow Ground, and upon the side of the neck of the Bottle our Name and Trade Mark in Letters coloured Black on a ground coloured Red in Opaque colouring; on the reverse side of the Capsule the Makers' name, Betts & Co., London. Feeling quite assured that this Capsule will protect our Customers' and our own interests, and therefore enhance the value of our Stout in every Market.

The letter included three coloured illustrations of the new closure and was a serious attempt at combating deception at a time when the laws governing authenticity were difficult to enforce. If Portugal seemed an unlikely setting for spurious Guinness, then the English port of Liverpool certainly was not. The sea link between this city and Dublin made it a home from home for immigrant Irishmen who pined for their native brew, and a number of fraudulent cases occurred here. For some strange reason, the inland Scottish whisky town of Kilmarnock was also tied in with a Guinness forgery, as was Cookstown in County Tyrone. But Guinness's caught up with John Doris, a wine and spirits merchant from Cookstown, who had issued a spurious signature-bearing Guinness's Extra label in brown monochrome which stated:

This is to certify that J. Doris deals exclusively with us for Porter and gets nothing but XX.

The Dublin brewery were able to extract a public apology from Doris admitting a contravention of their rights:

I hereby tender to Messrs Arthur Guinness, Son, and Company, Limited, an unqualified apology for having made use of a Bottle Label bearing a certificate purporting to have been given by Arthur Guinness, Son, and Company, which certificate I now state was never given to me

And I further undertake not again to use said Bottle Label, and have returned all copies thereof, together with the Blocks from which same were printed, to the said Arthur Guinness, Son, and Company, Limited, to be destroyed, and I give them full liberty to publish this apology in any papers they think desirable, the expenses whereof I undertake to pay.

Dated 11th day of October, 1886.

(Signed),

JOHN DORIS,

Of Cookstown.

Arthur Guinness,
Son, and Co., Limited,
St. James's Gate, Dublin.

The three-piece cylindrically shaped beer bottle with its horizontal shoulder seam and seam-free body did much to enhance the colourful paper labels being used from the 1870s onwards, for the advertising appendages could now be stuck on without their surfaces being impaired by underlying glass ridges. Another method of avoiding seam marks was developed through the technique of turn-moulding, which had been patented by a man called Evinson in the April of 1879. This involved coating the inside of the mould with plumbago (graphite) and tallow (beef- or mutton-fat), thus facilitating easy bottle rotation. This enabled containers to be turned during the making process, the operation successfully removing all trace of joins. With the coming of labelling machines in the 1870s, many glass bottles were produced in this way, particularly those used by the wine trade. The beer industry, as already mentioned, preferred to hedge its bets and continued to emboss its containers as well as to label them. Corks and ebonite screw stoppers also became an increasingly manipulated target for embossment and printing in the concluding years of Victoria's reign, both forms of closure having their own paper seals bearing such legends as 'Replace the stopper when empty' and 'Observe that this label is unbroken'.

Even in an age notorious for its erroneous use of royal patronage in advertising, no brewery worth its salt would have attempted to exploit the name or picture of Queen Victoria to sell its alcoholic beverages. Medicines, inks, edible pastes, toothpastes, mineral waters and confectioneries had all claimed patronage from royalty throughout the

work people, and even set up a board of trustees to ensure its correct management. The Kenwood estate and mansion adjoining London's Hampstead Heath was just one of the many gifts given to the British nation by the Guinness family. But perhaps above all, the breweries provided employment for a great many people.

The outstanding feature of Victorian beer was that it could be manufactured easily from four basic ingredients: barley, which having been converted into malt gave the brew body; hops, a later ingredient discovered by the Dutch, which imparted bitterness and redolence whilst protecting from infection; water, the chemical content of which had a profound effect on the brew's character and accounted for more than ninety per cent of its total content; yeast, a mass of minute vegetable cells which acted to provide alcohol.

Although it no longer applies, there was indeed a distinction in nineteenth-century Britain between ale and beer. Originally, ale was manufactured simply with malt, but beer required the addition of hops. The brewing process converted barley into malt by steeping it in water and allowing it to germinate. It was then carefully dried to allow the brewer to make full use of its sugar content, a high starch volume and a relatively low yield of nitrogen being essential. The malt was eventually crushed by mills to become what the brewers called 'grist'. Hops were added to beer by the Dutch and Germans as far back as 1360, but it wasn't until the sixteenth century that Flemish hop growers settled in Kent, Sussex and Hampshire, Britain's main hop-growing regions. Although not an essential constituent of brewing, they acted as a precipitant through their tannin content, and provided resins and oils for flavour and aroma. The right water, of course, was essential and often played an important part in deciding the locality of breweries. Burton-on-Trent is an excellent example of such a water source, being comparatively free from impurities. The famous 'clear' or 'pale' ales owed much of their success to the gypsum or hydrous sulphate of lime content of the waters in the Trent Valley, and it was here that the great Victorian breweries of Bass, Ind Coope, Allsopp and Worthington produced sparkling pale ales which became famous as far away as Russia and the East Indies. The malt grist and hot liquor which, when mixed together in the mash tun, formed a sweet liquid known as 'wort' (pronounced 'wert'), required yeast to convert its sugar content into alcohol, different types and measures being employed according to the desired brew. After fermentation, the excess yeast which had foamed to the top or settled to the bottom, depending on the brew, was separated and the beer stored.

A noteworthy deterrent to the bottling (as opposed to casking) of beers in the early years of the nineteenth century, apart from the tax on glass, was the duty levied on the beverage. For the purpose of taxation, there was a division of beer into two classes: 'strong' which revenued 2s (10p) a barrel, and 'small' which coined 6d (2½p) a barrel. Apparently, one of the official excise tests to distinguish between the two categories, was to seat a man wearing leather breeches in a pool of beer for 30 minutes. The brew was pronounced 'strong' if the unfortunate man actually adhered to the floor when the half hour had elapsed. Another more praiseworthy method of determining the strength of a brew, possibly as far as excise men were concerned anyway, was to drink the stuff. The financial drawbacks to the bottling of beers were eventually removed later in the century, and thus produced a great demand for the champagne-shaped bottle with no defined shoulder point and the square-shouldered bottle. Both types were adopted in half pint, one pint and quart sizes.

One notable brewing innovation from the Victorian era was, of course, the pasteurisation of beer, a process which arrested fermentation by killing harmful bacteria and delaying the development of others. Pasteur had been studying injurious growths in beer from about 1865, showing that it was possible to attenuate the virulence of harmful micro-organisms by exposure to air. During the course of his research Pasteur visited a number of English breweries including, in September 1871, the Chiswell Street Brewery of Whitbread's where he studied beer ferments. His *Études sur la Bière*, published in 1876, proved conclusively that organisms stimulating fermentation in alcohol were contained in the air. This encouraged leading brewers to give serious consideration to establishing research and control laboratories for the microscopic study of yeast and other related bacteriological work.

Hygiene and skilled judgement had, to a certain extent, always played an important role when it came to the bottling or casking of good porter and ale. The best of the early Victorian brewers considered it most important that bottles and casks be clean, sweet and dry, and that corks should be sound and good. Bottles for the home trade were usually left for at least twenty-four hours before corking. Beers for export were left without closures for a minimum of three days, when they would be well corked and wired. Some malt liquors, when bottled, were initially loosely corked and tightened afterwards. They were kept for a period of twenty-four hours in cold stillage or immersed in cold water, their corks having been scalded to make them more elastic. Flat ale was revived by placing a few raisins or horse beans (a variety of broad bean grown for fodder) in each bottle, whilst pepper-corns were an effective way of preventing bottles from bursting. Coarse sugar, boiled in water and fermented with yeast, reputedly ripened beer in a day, but bottles had to be kept in a warm place. About three spoonfuls of the mixture, when added to each bottle with a couple of cloves, supposedly ripened the beer quickly for consumption. Should a cask of ale have been considered sour, some brewers would have added *capillaire*, an infusion of maiden-hair syrup flavoured with orange-water, and fermented it with yeast. Powdered chalk was also used for the same purpose. When settled, the ale could be bottled with a lump of sugar, and a clove placed in each vessel to prevent bursting.

The quality of beer had improved somewhat by the 1880s, and was able to compete strongly with alcoholic and non-alcoholic rivals. Stout sold at 3d ($1\frac{1}{2}$p) per imperial gill bottle, and 6d ($2\frac{1}{2}$p) for each imperial pint bottle. Bitter and pale (Burton) ales could be purchased for the same amount. Lemonade and soda water retailed at 3d ($1\frac{1}{2}$p) per bottle, and cider at 1s (5p) per gallon jar. Pint bottles of port, claret and sherry were in the region of 2s 6d ($12\frac{1}{2}$p) per pint, and champagne was about 4s (20p) per pint. Pubs usually advertised spirits by the glass; rum, gin and whisky at 4d (2p), and brandy at 6d ($2\frac{1}{2}$p). But by the turn of the century, as far as the working man at any rate was concerned, beer was best.

10
WINES
AND SPIRITS

Because many of the better-off Victorians tended to live somewhat elegant life-styles, it was hardly surprising that their sense of propriety included the drinking of good wines. So that whilst the accent throughout the eighteenth and early nineteenth centuries had been on the quantity of wine consumed rather than the quality, Victorians were by contrast assessed on the credibility of cellars containing only the best wines.

Wine had, of course, been bottled in free-blown shaft-and-globe glass containers in Britain as far back as the seventeenth century, although these rolled-lip, shoulder-sealed bottles in pale green glass were made specifically for the wealthy. The status-conscious nobility would send these bottles to their wine merchants, who in turn would fill them from casks. When the signing of the Methuen Treaty in 1703 favoured Portugal at the expense of France, port soon became the traditional beverage of the higher orders of English society. This saw the demise of onion-shaped bottles in favour of straight-sided cylindricals which could be more easily stored. The importation of wine in bottles was forbidden from 1728 onwards, however, in an attempt to prevent smuggling, and was not repealed until the beginning of the nineteenth century. By this time, the custom of sealing free-blown bottles was gradually giving way to the embossment of machine-moulded containers. Wine bottles manufactured in this way were sold by the Bristol glass-works of Henry Ricketts & Co in the 1820s, and had the firm's name embossed on their bases. Their uniformity and speed of production did much to eliminate the fraudulent measures of wine and spirits previously sold in all manner of bottles of questionable capacity.

Harvey's of Bristol were a firm quick to take advantage of this reputable standardisation. They had been in the shipping and wine business since the early 1780s, and finally emerged as John Harvey & Sons in 1871. By 1893 they had become a limited liability company, enjoying the advantages of Bristol's close ties with the wine trade and the glass-making industry. Indeed, John Methuen's Treaty with the

(*Left*) Assorted Victorian wine bottles, c 1890. Note internal 'kick-up' base, tallest 31cm
(*Author's collection*)

(*Right*) Shoulder sealed wine bottle, c 1850 (*Courtesy John Harvey & Sons Limited*)

King of Portugal led many Bristol men to settle in both Lisbon and Oporto, so that for many years the wines of Portugal dominated the scene in Bristol. Usually, vintners such as Harvey's saw to it that all bottled wines went into sound, clean and dry containers which were well corked. When bottled, the wines were stored in a cool cellar on their sides and in sawdust, to ensure that their cork closures were kept moist (and therefore expanded) to prevent leakage and fermentation.

J. R. Phillips & Co Ltd, also of Bristol, had been wine and spirit shippers since 1739, and by the middle of the nineteenth century were trading throughout Britain, Europe and Jamaica. When James Rouquet Phillips died in 1836 his sons, William and Augustus, carried on the business in spite of the fact that their views on running the company differed considerably. To overcome this problem, the brothers came to the unusual arrangement that each should manage the business alternately for a fortnight. Surprising as it may seem, the firm continued to make profits, which by the late 1850s had risen to more than £3,500 a year. Gladstone's reductions in duties on wines between 1860 and 1862 undoubtedly helped the firm's trade during that decade and the one that followed, so that by 1889 Phillips & Co had become one of Bristol's first private limited companies with a capital of £80,000. The company also had part shares in three trading vessels about this time, but these were relinquished in 1899. The end of Victoria's reign saw the company expanding their markets for a wide range of wines, spirits and alcoholic cordials, the latter of which had been brewed at home from herbs and spices in accordance with recipes handed down by word of mouth for generations. Some were taken neat, some mixed with other drinks, and some were much in demand for their medicinal qualities. 'Shrub Cordial', which is still marketed by the firm today, was made from rum, citrus juices and various herbs, and was a well known remedy for chest complaints. Celery-flavoured 'Lovage' (a name applied botanically to various umbelliferous herbs) was often drunk to alleviate rheumatism, whilst 'Surfeit Water' would settle a disturbed stomach. A Phillips' price list dated 1890 records sixteen cordials of the firm's compounding, and it is interesting to note that the most popular of them are still made and sold today. Phillips' 'Lime Juice' (fortified with rum as a preservative) was loaded aboard many ships sailing from Bristol as an anti-scorbutic. The company thus became associated with the word 'limey', a derisory American derivative of 'lime-juicer', and relating to English sailors who visited American (and Australian) ports and were seen to drink this scurvy-preventing beverage. The firm are now part of the Grants, Sandeman, Seagram Combine.

Large two-quart and four-quart stone bottles were in regular use throughout the 1880s and 1890s for spirits, but because of capacity for re-use are seldom found intact in Victorian dumps. Usually in white or buff, these handled spirit bottles could be purchased with a cork-mouth or were fitted to take either a vulcanite screw stopper or a stone stopper complete with washer. Many had retailer's names printed on their shoulders, and could also be bought with screw-in boxwood taps. Bourne of Derby, Pearson of Chesterfield, and Doulton of Lambeth and Burslem, manufactured thousands of these during the Victorian era.

Temperance, prohibition and high government taxation were undoubtedly three of the main reasons why medicinal alcoholic tonics, known as bitters, became so popular during the last forty years of the nineteenth century. In America, such beverages were put on the market as medicines to by-pass prohibition legislation. These laws, first introduced in Maine in 1846 and throughout many states thereafter,

(*Left*) Brown salt glazed 'Gemeinde Pullna Bitters' container with incised lettering, 20¾cm
(*Les Martin collection*)

(*Right*) Brown salt glazed 'Kiderlen's Freebooter Gin' bottle, 30½cm
(*Les Martin collection*)

made illegal the sale of intoxicating liquor. Ostensibly, bitters were sold to a spirit-starved public as cure-alls, and were impregnated with herbs, roots and barks. The most notable of these was angostura, an aromatic bark from South American trees used as a tonic and febrifuge. Dumps throughout the United States have yielded hundreds of elaborately-shaped and embossed bitters containers since bottle collecting became fashionable there in the 1960s. Appetising trade names abounded, including 'Paw-paw', 'Apple Brandy', 'Trinidad Aromatic', 'Hop', 'Orange', 'Vegetable Sherry', 'Wild Cherry' and 'Indian Herb Bitters'. Even H. H. Warner of 'Safe Cure' fame was known to be advertising his 'Safe Bitters' during the 1870s with considerable success.

Drinking was known to be on the increase among the British middle classes, and the Temperance League unhesitatingly placed the blame squarely on the shoulders of the country's doctors. It was claimed, for example, that the Victorian medical profession were liberally prescribing whisky, gin, brandy, hock and champagne for rheumatic, bronchial and kidney disorders, afflictions which in the long term tended to be aggravated rather than soothed or cured by such pre-scriptions. Habitual drinking seems to have reached such a pitch among the working classes in Britain in the 1860s and 1870s, that many firms were forced to include inebriation in their lists of rules and regulations posted on the shop floor. One such list from a North Staffordshire factory in 1868 read:

System of Fines

Rule 4 For drinking spirits or fermented liquors, or being intoxicated, or for bringing in malt liquors or spirits – Fine 1s 0d.

The majority of bitters bottles found in British dumps come embossed and in varying shades of greens and ambers. It is debatable, of course, whether they were purchased for their medicinal or alcoholic properties, although there are those who would suggest that little distinction could be found between the two if the point were to be argued philosophically. The fact remains, however, that the persistance and strength of Victorian temperance movements pressured respective governments into placing a high tax on spirits. Inevitably this forced manufacturers of whiskies and gins into disguising the taste and smell of their produce, but not its potency.

To all intents and purposes, bitters were liquors impregnated with wormwood (a perennial herb having bitter and tonic properties) or other similar plants with medicinal claims, and taken as stomachics to promote digestion or appetite. Doc Hartman's famous 'Peruvian Tonic', however, originally contained twenty per cent whiskey, and was just one example of a bitters beverage which enjoyed massive sales. As a vehicle for avoiding increased taxation on spirits, the bitters industry must have provided an extremely satisfactory loophole, for by the end of the 1890s a commanding number of bitters manufacturers were in existence throughout Great Britain. All manner of attractively labelled bottles began to appear, including those of Henry Davis & Co of Liverpool. Initially, the firm was listed in 1882 as ship store dealers, wine spirit and provision merchants, and agents for 'Royal Blend Whiskey' and 'Khoosh Bitters'. By 1844 the firm had moved to new premises at 12 Goree Piazzas, Liverpool, and were trading under the name of The Khoosh Tonic Bitters Co Ltd, their 'Lady on the Tiger' trade mark becoming quite well known among bitters drinkers.

Another established bitters manufacturer of this decade was the firm of A. E. Powell & Co of Swindon in Wiltshire. Their trade mark of a plant resembling a moonflower advertised the company's 'Moonseed Bitters' and was registered in 1888. This lunary symbol may have been a subtle way of thumbing a nose at authority, for moonshine was a term which referred to smuggled spirits, whilst Wiltshire legend gave the title of moonraker to someone who was foolish. Quackery was still very much alive at this time, although it was often difficult to distinguish genuine herbalistic attempts to cure from outright charlatanism. The following extracts from *Astill's Swindon Almanac & Trades Register* of 1888 and relating to Powell's 'Moonseed Bitters' are typical of advertising methods in vogue during that period. Certainly they provide an interesting insight into the usage of rather extravagant and flamboyant claims regarding cures, and also vitriolic attacks on anything which might, by comparison, further the promotion of a particular rival product:

MOONSEED BITTERS have saved thousands from untimely graves; and it may be affirmed, with all the force of thorough conviction, that it will in the future do even greater things, and that millions yet unborn will by its agency be healed of diseases under which, but for its powerful aid, they would sink. There is no disease known to humanity which it will not benefit . . . Its marvellous healing virtues do not admit of exaggerated praise. Nothing to equal them is recorded in the annals of Therapeutics, and it is as harmless as it is powerful. The compound is based on an extract of the Moonseed root, added to which are other choice and mighty healing roots and barks, all combined and compounded in certain exact proportions, known only to the proprietor, and discovered by him after years of study, research and experiment. MOONSEED BITTERS is infinitely more powerful and effective in its cleansing, healing and tonic action than any of the vaunted Bitters so widely advertised, and which are put forward as containing the most valuable portions of hops, buchu, dandelion, and mandrake, and "the purest and best medicinal properties of all other Bitters." These have been for years every old woman's prescription; but they are not to be compared for a moment with MOONSEED, a bottle of which is, as a medicine, worth a ton of other Bitters.

MOONSEED BITTERS is guaranteed to cure Cancer in its worst form, before and after amputation, if as large as the head of a two-pound loaf. All the inhabitants of Swindon know this. ASTHMA, CONSUMPTION, AND PARALYSIS POSITIVELY CURED.

The *North Wiltshire Directory* for 1889 included some of the 26,000 testimonials claimed to have been received by the makers of 'Moonseed Bitters' in praise of the mixture, together with disparaging attacks on the medical fraternity:

> It is strange, and, at first sight, an inexplicable circumstance, that in these days of enlightenment – in the closing years of the nineteenth century – when science is making such gigantic strides, and discoveries are being almost daily made which revolutionise society, one science, that of medicine, should yet lag behind; and one art, that of healing, be yet still far from having obtained to even an approximate certainty of procedure . . . Why is it then that with all their boasted skill and learning, our medical men achieve so little? How is it that in spite of their noxious drugs, their poisons, their bleedings and blisterings, disease so often gains the victory, and that thousands are swept away by maladies, which, if doctors knew their business, should be amenable to treatment? Must it not be that these men work on a false principle, or on no principle at all? . . . the noble art of healing has degenerated into professional quackery.

The article then goes on boldly to attack fraudulent advertising whilst at the same time listing, in a surprisingly comprehensive manner, a whole spectrum of ailments guaranteed to be cured by the imbibing of 'Moonseed Bitters':

> The greatest National Disease in this Country is Fraud. £1,000 IS THEREFORE GUARANTEED to anyone who will prove that Moonseed Bitters will not cure Consumption, Asthma, Bronchitis, Whooping Cough, Cough, Croop, Diptheria, Palpitation of the Heart, Liver Diseases, Indigestion, Gravel, Dropsy, Bright's and other Kidney Diseases, Worms, Piles, and all Morbid and Critical Discharges, Internal and External Cancers, Tumours and Ulcerations, and absolutely remove all unpleasant symptoms during Pregnancy, remove after pains, and render Puerperal Fever impossible; Full Necks, Abscesses, Scrofula, Glandular Swellings, Old Ulcerated Legs, Lupus, and every form of Skin and Blood Disease, Nervous Debility, Epilepsy, Neuralgia, Convulsions, Paralysis, &c., &c., Colic, Cramp, Wind, and Spasms relieved in three seconds. One bottle contains enough to cure from six to twenty-four children of whooping cough. It will absolutely cut off Fevers, and remove every symptom in three days. It is true that Divine Writ says "For the blood is the life," but it does not tell you to quack it by taking potass and chloroform. All wise people will avoid such stuff, together with arsenic and other vile and pernicious trash. Moonseed Bitters is the only reliable blood medicine that will stamp out all the above diseases, strengthen the brain, remove all pain, and insure sweet and refreshing sleep.

Undoubtedly the drinking of bitters did much good and cured many people of many ailments, but whether this was as a direct result of their ingredients or of the more subtle 'miracle' of mind over matter, is open to debate.

There seems little doubt that gin was the drink most favoured by the

Victorian working classes, although it must be remembered that a large percentage of sales depended almost wholly on point-of-sale advertising. In other words, until the 1870s, much of the gin sold in Britain was dispensed from casks in taverns and gin palaces and not sold in bottles. Dark flint-glass bottles, however, were used to export gin from Holland as early as the 1840s and had the distillers' names embossed on them. These earlier containers would have been free-blown and have had base pontil marks, but by the 1860s the Schiedam distillers were using the now familiar mould-blown tapered-bodied case-gins. These short-necked olive green containers were exported to Britain in specially-made wooden cases, thus acquiring the generic title of 'case-gins'.

Originally distilled in the 1650s for medicinal purposes by Professor Sylvius, a Leyden doctor, gin was made from rye and flavoured with berries from the prickly evergreen shrub juniper. The spirit proved so palatable, that apothecaries were manufacturing it in large quantities, and as a hard liquor rather than a medicine. British mercenaries fighting for the Dutch were known to have taken gin or 'Dutch courage' before going into battle, and were probably responsible for introducing it to the British Isles. It was sold as a cure-all by English chemists during the second half of the eighteenth century when the Gin Act of 1736, with its high duty of twenty shillings a gallon, drove it under-ground in much the same way as later Acts did with other spiritous beverages.

The majority of Victorian refuse tips yield reasonable quantities of these beautifully shaped and coloured case-gins, and most collectors will have at least one (probably unembossed) such container to their credit. That Holland held complete dominance of the gin trade in Britain throughout Victoria's reign does not detract from the fact that British distillers, particularly those in London and Plymouth, were extremely active from the 1860s onwards. Newspaper advertisements from this period relate to a number of famous names including Pimm & Co, Tanqueray & Co, Gordon & Co, Gilbey & Co, Coates & Co, and Boord & Son. The Boord family can be traced back to the reign of Richard II, and came from Bristol. They certainly were maltsters in Bristol in the eighteenth century, but by Victoria's reign had established themselves as distillers in London. The famous 'Cat & Barrel' trade mark was designed and registered by Joseph Boord in 1849 and was one of the earliest recorded in the gin industry of England. Infringe-ments appear to have been frequent, for not only did the company have to fight transgression actions in Britain, but overseas as well. Towards the turn of the century, Boord's had a considerable trade with the

(*Left*) Victorian case-gin, 23½cm; (*right*) modern Dutch 'Bokma' gin bottle
(*Author's collection*)

Lord Brougham, John Bull and Daniel O'Connell stoneware spirit flasks (*Courtesy Denby Tableware Limited*)

United States, and in 1898 alone obtained over twenty high-court injunctions (including costs) against infringing companies in California.

The emergence of the Distillers Co Ltd in 1877 eventually saw the merging of a number of established distilleries throughout Britain including Boord, Buchanan and Booth. The latter family, the most senior of London's gin distilling companies, came from the north east of England in the seventeenth century. By the middle of the following century they were established distillers, and by 1778 were operating from a site only a few hundred yards from their present Red Lion Distillery in Clerkenwell. An example of the firm's benevolence can be seen in the personal financing by Felix Booth of the second expedition of Sir John Ross in 1829 to find the legendary North West Passage. As a result, Ross discovered the peninsula 'Boothia Felix' and the Gulf of Boothia, which now form part of the 3,400,000 square kilometres of Canada's North West Territories. Fragments of Booth's spirit bottles have been found as far away as Tasmania, their cask-mellowed 'House of Lords' gin being just one of their liquors which was well received throughout Victoria's vast empire.

The Black Friars Distillery belonging to Coates & Co of Plymouth was formerly a monastery for Dominican monks, becoming linked with the distillation of gin in the latter part of the eighteenth century. To guard against spurious imitations of their universally reputed 'Plymouth Gin', Coates & Co would never allow their spirit to be exported in casks for re-bottling. The firm's produce was thus shipped in wooden cases containing bottles handled entirely by staff at the Plymouth distillery. The glass containers, bearing labels depicting the robed figure of a Dominican friar, a trade mark first used in 1793, were filled, corked, capsuled, labelled, wrapped and packed in cases exclusively by Coates' employees. An extract from a Victorian analyst's certificate denoting the merits of Coates' 'Plymouth Gin' read:

> I have subjected the sample of gin from your distillery to a most careful chemical and physiological analysis. I find it to be an absolutely pure spirit, with an extremely fine gin or geneva flavour, an agreeable stimulant and a wholesome dietetic. The purity of this gin is so absolute that it retains its specific gravity after distillation and reduction to its previous bulk, and leaves no extractive, particularly no saccharine matter in the residue. It is perfectly free from fused oil, or any of the empyreumatic substances which not rarely impair the flavour and diminish the dietetic value of certain kinds of new and so-called raw spirits.

Because the drinking of gin was not considered socially acceptable in upper-class Victorian households, this does not mean that it was not taken in private. Hypocrisy was even carried to the extreme by some well-to-do families, who had silver labels engraved with the word 'nig' specially made to hang on their gin decanters. The implication here, of course, was that they did not wish their servants to know that their 'betters' had succumbed to the traditional drink of the working classes. Although there remains a great deal of evidence which suggests that gin was the scourge of the poor in Victorian England, it could be argued that it was far safer to drink 'Mother's Ruin' than to rely on contaminated water supplies. Considering the appalling conditions to which the working classes were subjected, it was little wonder that so many sought short-term release in the gin palaces of the day.

Probably the greatest social evil to stem from the unrestrained consumption of gin was the widespread habit of feeding it to babies and young children. Mothers, having worked a tiring twelve-hour day in the factory, were only too willing to dose their tiny infants to sleep, thus enabling them to escape to the local dram shop and blot out (if only for a short while) the problems of life. Working mothers were also in the habit of putting very young babies into the care of a wet-nurse. Many of these old women were habitual gin drinkers living in damp, airless cellars who did not hesitate to give these wretched children a tipple or an opium and treacle-soaked rag to suck to keep them quiet. Chimney-sweeps, whose custom it was to employ only boys of small stature as human flue-brushes, were reputed to have forced these luckless youngsters (most of them orphans from work-houses) to drink a good deal of gin in the belief that it would retard their growth. The implications are almost too horrifying to contemplate. How much the infant mortality in Victorian times was due to children being drugged and poisoned in this way is anyone's guess, but in retrospect the indications seem staggering.

The production of gin followed three important stages. The primary process, involving the manufacture of the raw spirit, was attained by traditional methods of fermentation and distillation. The secondary stage saw the basic spirit being rectified through a complicated system of stills until a pure, colourless liquid emerged. The final or tertiary process (the precise portion of the 'run' having been decided upon) involved the careful introduction of the flavouring ingredients. The most universally appealing ingredient was juniper, and it was the dark, oily and aromatic berries of this evergreen shrub which complemented so perfectly the pure alcohol and provided the basic flavouring for such famous London gins as Gordon's, Charles Tanqueray's, and others. Sloe gin flavoured with the small, dark-purple fruits of the blackthorn also proved extremely popular with British drinkers, and

'Ye Olde Cheshire Cheese' whisky jug, 23cm (*Les Martin collection*)

when Gordon and Tanqueray formed themselves into a limited liability company in 1898 under the name of Tanqueray, Gordon & Co Ltd, they were supplying such spirits in bulk to various categories of customers. These distillations were to include gins flavoured with orange and lemon as well as the traditional juniper, and were 'broken down' by the retailer to the required strength for dispensing. Dispensing usually took place from bulk containers of various types, depending upon the establishments in question. It was not until the turn of the century, incidentally, that demand grew for a supply of gin in branded bottles. Indeed, the world famous Tanqueray and Gordon brand image of a boar's head began to appear in the late 1890s (the device, of course, goes back much further), although bottles were not generally available at this time and labels very much dependant upon individual outlets.

Although London was perhaps rightly regarded as the principal seat of gin production in Victorian England (the first gin palace is thought to have been in Holborn Hill), it was in no way true that the metropolis had a monopoly of the industry. Excellent gins were produced outside the Wen at some of the old market towns including, for example, Bunting's 'Fine Sloe Gin' from Uttoxeter, Ffennell's 'Bullfinch Brand' sloe gin from Brighton's Western Road, Bernard's slightly sweetened 'Old Tom' gin from their Leith distillery, and 'XXXX' gin rectified by A. A. Watt & Co of Ship Quay Street,

Cambus Distillery (*Courtesy DCL*)

Londonderry. The firm of Watt & Co was founded in 1762 and also produced selected blends of 'Tyrconnell Whisky', but these family-owned distilleries are now defunct. An interesting part of the firm's tradition was that each day the left-over samples of spirit were poured into a large, dark glass bottle of the wide-based, shaft-necked variety. This container stood about two feet high, and drivers were allowed to help themselves from the mixture – a worthwhile bonus.

Very few United Kingdom distilleries outside London earned the wide and substantial reputation enjoyed by the makers of 'Pulling's Gin'. This Hereford distillery was established in 1813, the company still operating as Pulling & Co Ltd, Wine Merchants, from the town's St Peter's Square. Like all distilleries in the 1890s, the firm's stills were heated by fire, and could only be used by giving twenty-four hours notice to the Excise Authorities. The larger of their two ancient stills was used for rectifying the spirit, and the smaller one for compounding the various flavouring ingredients. The application of heat to the stills caused their contents to pass off in vapour through the 'heads' or necks, which were connected with the coils of a 'worm', to a huge tub. The worm was submerged in cold water, and as the vapour penetrated

Cameronbridge Distillery (*Courtesy DCL*)

through the coils, it was condensed into spirit and flowed through copper safes into receivers. This process was repeated until the spirit was completely rectified, and it was then run from the worm into huge vats beneath the floor of the still-house. From these vats, the gin was pumped into smaller tanks in the spirit store where it could be run off into casks or bottles as required. Pulling's, however, did not only specialise in gin, for by the turn of the century they had the largest bonded and duty-paid wine and spirit trade in Herefordshire. Their East Street premises in 1893 contained (apart from gin) vats for whisky, brandy, rum, cordials and liqueurs of various kinds. There was a champagne vault, and beyond this a port-bottling vault around which pipes (large wine casks usually containing 150 gallons) of Martinez's, Sandeman's and other famous ports were ranged on stillages. The sherry-bottling vault had butts of choice wines from the principal Spanish bodegas, whilst a bin vault was stocked with old vintage ports, sherries, Madeiras and hocks. Another large vault had clarets in wood occupying the scantlings, and clarets in bottles filling the bins; this in turn led to a special vault binned with various growths and vintages of Burgundy. All these were duty-paid goods, and provide some indication of the extent of the company's comprehensive stocks.

Kirkliston Distillery (*Courtesy DCL*)

It is sometimes thought, erroneously, that the stoneware reform flasks so much in evidence at the beginning of Victoria's reign and so prized by today's collectors, were designed to cater for the needs of those wishing to appear to subscribe to the condemnation of gin and other spirits by social reformers. Nothing, in fact, was farther from the truth, for whilst they were both related to a striving after respectability, the Reform Act of the 1830s had very little to do with temperance. In the event, the Act extended the franchise to the middle but not (as was hoped) to the working classes. This improvement of the electoral and parliamentary systems in Great Britain, however, opened the floodgates to a host of remedial movements which were now able to concentrate upon parliamentary action as the means to reform. The avalanche of improvement-seeking Bills that followed, invariably established the draughtsmen of the first Reform Act as public crusaders. Lord Brougham, although unpopular with his colleagues, had been an idol of the people since the early twenties; Sir Francis Burdett was reputed to be the most popular English politician of his time; Lord Grey was the Whig leader; Lord Russell was the fourth member of the government entrusted with the task of framing the Reform Bill and of proposing it.

Carsebridge Distillery (*Courtesy DCL*)

It probably came as no surprise, then, that thousands of specially designed spirit-flasks and larger bottles (which eventually became known as 'Reform bottles' and 'Reform flasks') were manufactured by firms like Doulton & Watts, Joseph Bourne and Pearson. Many of the vessels bore the heads of the men directly connected with the Bill, and carried appropriate slogans such as the ambiguous 'The True Spirit of Reform' and 'Reform Cordial'. Cordial in those days, incidentally, was an aromatised and sweetened spirit, and not some innocuous dilutable syrup or fruit juice. A bottle-shaped Lord Grey could be obtained with a tightly-clutched scroll bearing the inscription 'The Peoples Rights', whilst the bewigged head and squared shoulders of Lord Russell formed the neck and shoulders of a companion bottle. Daniel O'Connell, the fiery Irish political leader, was also immortalised in this way, as was William IV for possibly different reasons. The 'sailor king' had been a Whig up to his accession, when he turned Tory. It was well known that William did much to obstruct the passage of the first Reform Act, the passing of which led, along with other great changes, to the abolition of colonial slavery and the reforming of the poor-laws. Perhaps in the light of this, Victoria's uncle was included in the series as a figure to be scorned rather than esteemed.

Stoneware bottles were ideally suited for whisky and were commonly used for export because of their durability. They could also be easily transfer-printed, which overcame the difficulty of finding paper labels capable of withstanding the rigours of long-distance shipping. These earthenware containers were often subject to less customs duty than their glass counterparts and hence found their way in great numbers into Australian refuse dumps of the nineteenth century. Such stoneware spirit jars were used by the old Irish whiskey firm of Mitchell's from Belfast to export their liquor, and many of these containers bearing the company's name and the words 'Cruiskeen Lawn' have come to light in dumps the other side of the world. Such jugs, which range in height from approximately ten centimetres to twenty-two centimetres, have black transfer-printing on cream bodies and carry the potter's marks of Mayland's, Kennedy & Sons and Port Dundas. The transfer includes the words 'Old Irish Whisky' surmounted by the imperial crown, and the majority of jugs incorporate a tan coloured neck.

Whiskey was Irish in origin and derived its name from the Gaelic 'uisge-beatha' which meant the water of life. It was likely that the spirit first came to Scotland from Ireland, although Scotch whisky was distilled from malt, as opposed to Irish whiskey (the 'e' is now commonly used to describe the spirit when distilled outside Scotland) which came from barley. American whiskey was based on Indian corn or rye, and became known through the States as bourbon because it originated in Bourbon County, Kentucky. Scotland, however, with its home-grown cereals and pure burn waters which combined to produce whisky of unique flavour, had established its industry so firmly through-out the world during the second half of the nineteenth century that when Victoria died in 1901 it was without rival. The Queen, who always had a passionate regard for Scottish tradition, made certain that her households were well stocked with whisky, and that it be made available to all her servants at the celebrating of great events. Towards the end of her life, Victoria ensured that a full bottle of Scotch be always at the disposal of her favourite gillie, John Brown, who when he died at Windsor in 1883 had been her personal attendant for thirty-four years.

The Victorians were accustomed to two basic types of Scotch whisky. There was the pure malt which was produced mainly in the Highlands in pot-stills from malted barley alone, and there was the grain produced from a mixture of malted and unmalted cereals. The introduction of Aeneas Coffey's patent-still in the 1830s was an innovation quickly seized upon by Lowland distillers, for it had the advantage of being able to distil whisky in one continuous operation. Unlike the traditional

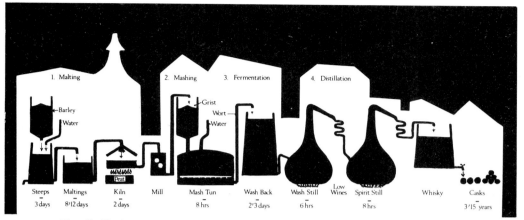

Steeps	Maltings	Kiln	Mill	Mash Tun	Wash Back	Wash Still	Low Wines	Spirit Still	Whisky	Casks
— 3 days	— 8/12 days	— 2 days		— 8 hrs	— 2/3 days	— 6 hrs		— 8 hrs		— 3/15 years

1. Malting   2. Mashing   3. Fermentation   4. Distillation

The distillation process of malt whisky (*Courtesy John Walker & Sons Limited*)

Port Dundas Distillery (*Courtesy DCL*)

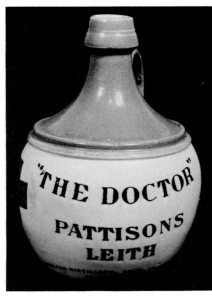

(*Left*) Chrystal, Bell & Co whisky bottle (*Courtesy Arthur Bell & Sons Limited*)
(*Centre*) Dewar whisky jug, 1897, 20⅓cm (*Dewar collection*)
(*Right*) Pattisons 'The Doctor' whisky jug, 19cm (*Les Martin collection*)

pot-still, which was heated by a furnace and had to be emptied and then refilled, the Coffey still was heated by steam, and because it was continuous had a much greater output. The obvious economic advantages of large-scale production saw the increased adaptation of the patent-still among grain whisky distillers, and many went out of business in the 1850s when over-production resulted in trade recessions. Up until the 1870s, distillers would sell their product to wholesale merchants, who then made up the proprietory brands. Grain whisky was light in flavour and body, and the layman could detect very little difference between the spirituous liquor produced by any number of patent stills. Malt whisky, on the other hand, could be termed more redolent, the strong single malts of individual distilleries being matured longer and having distinct flavours of their own.

In an endeavour to produce a blend of whisky acceptable to most palates, old malts began to be mixed with younger distillations and the more strongly flavoured whiskies (as for example from Skye) blended with softer varieties such as those from Speyside. It was, of course, a natural progression to blend malt and grain whiskies, probably the first firm to attempt this being that of Usher in the 1860s. The process was quickly taken up on a large scale by other leading distilleries, so that the whisky destined to become so popular south of the border was essentially a blend of grain and malt.

Because many of the early grain distillers collapsed in the recession which followed the introduction of Coffey's patent-still, a trade agreement was entered into by some of the leading companies in an attempt to protect their common interests and to reduce the risk of slumps caused by over-production. This was in 1856, and was followed within twenty years by the combining of six Lowland grain whisky distilleries: Robert Moubray's Cambus Distillery, John Haig & Co's Cameronbridge Distillery, John Bald & Co's Carsebridge Distillery, McNab Bros & Co's Glenochil Distillery, Stewart & Co's Kirkliston Distillery and, with an annual output of 2,502,000 proof gallons, the Port Dundas Distillery of D. Macfarlane & Co, the largest of its kind in Scotland. This then was the beginning of The Distillers Co Ltd, a powerful organisation formed in 1877 from old-established firms with hundreds of years of experience in the whisky trade between them.

From the 1860s, French vineyards suffered greatly from the spread of phylloxera, an insect pest native to North America which attacked grape vines and laid its eggs under the bark, the resulting devastation forcing brandy to yield pride of place to blended Scotch whisky as the drink of the Victorian upper and middle classes. This shift of public taste owed much to the arrival on the London scene of some young Scotsmen of extraordinary commercial ability whose famous names were later to be included in the Distillers combine.

Alexander Walker of Kilmarnock established a London office in 1880. His father, John Walker, had purchased a grocery, wine and spirits business in Kilmarnock's King Street in 1820, and buyers attracted to the town by the growing textiles and engineering trades frequently developed a taste for Walker's brand of Kilmarnock whisky. Young Alexander brought to the firm the exciting concept of wholesale trading on a wide scale, for he was fully aware that the local retailing trade could be the foundation of a much more widely-based home market enterprise. He was also an enthusiastic supporter of the merchant venturer system, whereby goods were entrusted to the captain of a ship who would sell them to overseas markets on commission at the best price he could get. Hence the origins of Walker's vast overseas markets can be accredited to Alexander's hard work and foresight. So rapid in fact was the development of John Walker & Sons that a bottling hall was opened in London a few months after the firm's office there, and by 1893 the ever-increasing demand for their products saw the company acquire the famous Cardow Distillery in Speyside, which is still an important part of the Walker operation.

James Buchanan, another of the Scotch whisky trade's bright young men, was born in Brockville, Western Canada, and educated privately in Northern Ireland. He began his business life as an office boy, graduated to the position of clearing clerk, and by the age of nineteen had joined his brother as a grain merchant. His first direct link with the Scotch whisky trade was at the age of thirty when he came to London in the autumn of 1879 to act as an agent for a Leith whisky house. In something less than five years, James Buchanan had founded his own business, and by 1889 he had entered his 'Buchanan Blend' at the Paris Exhibition and been awarded the gold medal for blended whisky. In 1898 Buchanan bought the Old Swan Distillery at Holborn for £87,000 and in the same year both Queen Victoria and the Prince of Wales (later Edward VII) bestowed the royal warrant on the firm. In the previous year, Buchanan had purchased his own Highland malt distillery, Glentauchers-Glenlivet, at Mulben on Speyside, to ensure that regular supplies of perfect Highland malt liquor be available for his blends. In the early years of Edward's reign, James Buchanan & Co was incorporated as a limited liability company, the firm going on to acquire the Highland Convalmore Distillery at Dufftown, the Lowland Bankier Distillery, and a majority interest in the whisky firm of W. P. Lowrie & Co.

Thomas R. Dewar also set up his London office in 1884, the firm opening their first provincial branch at Bristol ten years later. Established in Perth as a wine and spirit merchants in 1846, Dewar & Sons were reputed to be the first distillers in Scotland to sell whisky in bottles under their own name. This, however, was in the 1870s. In 1855 Dewar's whisky had won the Edinburgh Exhibition Gold Medal and begun to establish itself actively in the export trade. The blend (known as 'White Label' abroad) never varied due to its being based on so many matured malts, for the firm owned distilleries at Aberfeldy in Perth, Lochnagar in Aberdeen, Muir of Ord in Ross-shire, Pulteney in Wick, and Aultmore, Parkmore and Benrinnes in Banffshire.

The distinction between malt distillers, grain distillers and blenders had lessened considerably by the 1890s, and blenders such as Buchanan, Dewar and Walker were beginning to acquire their own malt distilleries. The Mackies, who had begun as malt distillers at Lagavulin (a couple of miles east of Port Ellen) on the Isle of Islay, had produced a single malt whisky there from as far back as the 1740s. An old Stirlingshire family, they had owned property in Edinburgh for generations, but it was Peter Mackie who was ultimately responsible for entering the market for blended whisky with the firm's 'White Horse' brand in the 1880s. The Haigs too had been connected with distilling from the early 1600s, the family owning distilleries at Kilbagie,

Kennetpans, Tullian, Canonmills, Lochrin, Sunbury, Bonnington, Seggie and Dodderbank (near Dublin) down the years. Probably the best known of the Haig distilleries, however, was that of Cameronbridge, built on a fourteen-acre site at Windygates in Fife by John Haig in 1822. Although John Haig & Co merged their grain whisky distillery in The Distillers Co Ltd in 1876, they nevertheless (being whisky dealers as well as distillers) elected to retain their dealer's business, transfer it to Markinch some three miles west of Cameronbridge and carry it on as a separate enterprise. The boom years of the 1890s saw the structure of the Scotch whisky industry change out of all recognition as new companies were promoted and new distilleries built.

When the Leith blending company, Pattisons Ltd, suspended payment on 6 December 1898, the collapse reverberated through the whole whisky trade and the boom was turned into a recession. Investors and speculators expecting fat profits lost everything, and within the next ten years some forty distilleries were forced to close down. By the turn of the century the Pattison brothers, Robert and Walter, had been tried and convicted of fraud, the firm's Ballindalloch Distillery in Banffshire and its premises in Leith's Bernard Street were in liquidation, and The Distillers Co Ltd were more convinced than ever before that their policy of amalgamation was the best form of protection against the dangers of over-production. The famous Pattisons Whisky advertisement showing a British ironclad (a warship) with a kilted highlander figure-head and the slogan 'Forging Ahead' took on ironic overtones when the company crashed, as did the claim that 'Pattisons Whisky, like a British ironclad, is at home in all waters'.

Not all the famous names in the whisky industry were members of large consortiums, however, and some survived the pressures of the late Victorian era as independent establishments. Arthur Bell & Sons Ltd was such a company, having been established in Perth, the ancient capital of Scotland, in 1825. It was founded by Thomas Sandeman as a whisky merchant's shop in the city's Kirkgate, Arthur Bell joining the firm as a salesman in the early 1840s a few years after Sandeman's death. The archetypal Victorian industrialist, Bell was soon working out his own blends from the various malt and grain whiskies available through numerous small and privately owned distilleries in Scotland at that time. Oddly enough he was not a great believer in advertising and was of the opinion that no useful purpose would be served by putting his own brand name on his bottles of Scotch or selling his casks of whisky under a specific mark of distinction. His sons, Arthur Kinmond Bell and Robert Bell, however, were anxious to expand the business, and realised that the quickest way to attain this end was through advertising and the adoption of brand names. Thus, when he died in 1900, Arthur Bell left behind him a thriving family whisky concern the profits of which had doubled in the last five years of his life.

William Teacher began in business by selling off-licence whisky in Glasgow's Cheapside Street in the 1830s. Twenty-five years later the Teacher family held eighteen licences in Glasgow and its surrounding districts, and now sold whisky which could be drunk on the premises. By the middle of the nineteenth century, William had become a wholesale wine and spirit merchant, the firm undertaking serious blending in 1865 when large blending vats and a bottling plant were installed at their new premises in St Enock Square. In 1897 twenty-one years after the founder's death, Teacher's started to build from scratch their modern Ardmore Distillery near Kennethmont in Aberdeenshire. Set in superb barley-producing countryside and with an excellent supply of clear burn water, this malt distillery made it possible for the firm to control the most important ingredient of its blends.

Ireland, too, had its fair share of champions when it came to the distillation and blending of whiskey. Firms like Watts of Londonderry and Mitchell's of Belfast have already been mentioned, but Kinahan's 'LL' blend took the Dublin Prize Medal at the Dublin Exhibition of 1856 for the Northern Ireland company Kinahan's 'LL' Irish whiskey retailed at 3s 8d (18p) per bottle in mid-nineteenth-century Britain, the containers having red seals, pink labels, and corks branded with the words 'Kinahan's LL Whiskey'. Another well known Irish malt whiskey was that of Falkner's, a firm established in Dublin in 1780. Victorians could purchase Falkner's seven years old 'Real Malt' for the enviable price of 20s (£1) per gallon, and a ten years old malt for 22s (£1.10) per gallon.

Bushmills whiskey, or at least the bottles which contained it, are quite familiar to today's collectors. These square but rather petite glass containers carry the embossment of a still, and are fairly common in one pint and half-pint sizes. The distillery at Bushmills in County Antrim is thought to have been established in 1704, but it was not until 1887 that the firm opened a head office in Belfast and became registered as The Old Bushmills Distillery Company. 'Old Bushmills' with its superb golden colour was made from a blend of malt whiskey from the Old Bushmills Distillery and Coleraine grain whiskey. Possibly because it was based on the type of whisky produced in Scotland (blended grain and malt), 'Old Bushmills' proved successful in the face of fierce competition from poteen (illicitly distilled whiskey) when other Irish distillers were hard pressed to survive. The Boyd family, who had owned

'Coffin' and 'pumpkin seed' whisky bottles, tallest 20cm (*Author's collection*)

the Old Bushmills Distillery since 1884, eventually sold it to Great Universal Stores. The distillery was acquired by the Bass-Charrington Group in 1964, who also owned the old established wine and spirit merchants, Lyle and Kinahan, and the Ulster Brewery Co. Since 1972, the distillery has been owned jointly by the Canadian Seagram Group and the Irish Distillers Co Ltd.

'Coffin flasks' and 'pumpkin seeds' adorn the shelves of most bottle collectors, for they were popular containers for whisky in the late nineteenth century and are regularly found in dumps which can be dated to this period. Not unnaturally, coffin flasks acquired the nickname because of their round-shouldered and tapering shape. Manufacturers of Scotch whisky (and of Irish whiskey too for that matter), availed themselves mainly of glass bottles for the home trade, coffins and pumpkin seeds being supplied largely to hotels and inns and embossed with the name of the retailer and his premises. In Victorian times, except for the latter period, spirits were almost entirely a bulk business. The customer either bought from the cask by tot (a small measure of liquor) in the public house or, when purchasing for home consumption, sent to the tavern a servant, or child, according to his

(*Left*) 'Champagne' shape stoneware whisky bottle, 21½cm (*Les Martin collection*)

(*Centre*) Dewar's 'Perth' whisky jug, 30½cm (*Harry Haddon collection*)

(*Right*) 'The Fair Maid of Perth' whisky jug, 24cm (*Dewar collection*)

social position, with a suitable container: hence the 'Jug & Bottle' section still to be seen in some residual Victorian inns. Indeed, publicans tended to keep a stock of empty pint and half-pint whisky bottles specifically for customers wishing to purchase off-licence spirits. The Magee Marshall brands of 'Number 10 Liqueur Whisky' and 'Old Sou'wester Rum' are typical examples of coffin flasks known to collectors throughout the North and Midlands, whilst literally hundreds of pumpkin seed whisky bottles embossed with local retailers' names exist. Larger half-gallon glass whisky jugs with glass swing stoppers are also known to have been manufactured in the 1890s by Dan Rylands of Barnsley and others, although stoneware flasks and jugs tended to be more popular in Ireland and Scotland when it came to exporting to North America and Australia.

Stoneware whisky jugs for the export market were preferred mainly because of their underglaze transfer-printing. The damp hold conditions aboard ships undertaking long sea voyages were hardly conducive to paper labels, which tended to fall off en route. Several Scottish potbanks supplied the Scotch whisky trade with stoneware jars from the 1860s onwards, including Buchan of Portobello near Edinburgh and Cochran, Govancroft (who also made attractively collectable stoneware footwarmers and hot water bottles), Grosvenor Potteries, Kennedy and Port Dundas, all of Glasgow.

BIBLIOGRAPHY

Ball, A. *Collecting Pot-lids*, M.A.B. Publishing, Burton on Trent, 1977

Beck, D. *The Book of Bottle Collecting*, Hamlyn, London, 1973

Burton, E. *The Early Victorians at Home*, Allen Lane, London, 1974

Cousins, G. E. *A Family of Spirit*, W. Teacher & Sons, Glasgow, 1975

Covill Jr, W. E. *Ink Bottles & Inkwells*, William S. Sullwold, Taunton, Massachusetts, 1971

Dale, R. *Price Guide to Black & White Pot Lids*, A.C.C., Woodbridge, Suffolk, 1977

Doxat, J. *Booth's Handbook of Cocktails & Mixed Drinks*, Pan Books, London, 1966

Dyes, H. J. *The Victorian Suburb*, Leicester University Press, Leicester, 1966

Fletcher, E. *Antique Bottles in Colour*, Blandford, Poole, Dorset, 1974

Fletcher, E. *Collecting Pot Lids*, Pitman, London, 1975

Fletcher, E. *Digging Up Antiques*, Pitman, London, 1975

Genders, R. *A History of Scent*, Hamish Hamilton, London, 1972

Gregg, P. *A Social & Economic History of Britain*, Harrap, London, 1973

Hadfield, C. *British Canals*, David & Charles, Newton Abbot, 1974

House, J. *Pride of Perth*, Hutchinson Benham, London, 1976

Janes, H. *The Red Barrel*, Watney Mann, London, 1963

Kennett, F. *History of Perfume*, Harrap, London, 1975

Langbridge, R. H. (Ed.) *Life in the 1870s*, Times Books, London, 1974

Lochhead, M. *The Victorian Household*, John Murray, London, 1964

Martin, L. *A Collector's Guide to Olde Whisky Jugs*, Martin & Packham, London, 1977

Mathias, P. *The Retailing Revolution*, Allied Suppliers, Hayes, Middlesex, 1967

Meigh, E. *The Story of the Glass Bottle*, Ramsden, Stoke on Trent, 1972

Munsey, C. *The Illustrated Guide to Collecting Bottles*, Hawthorn Books, New York, 1970

Pike, E. R. *Human Documents of the Age of the Forsytes*, Allen & Unwin, London, 1969

Reader, W. J. *Life in Victorian England*, Batsford, London, 1964

Spiller, B. *Victorian Public Houses*, David & Charles, Newton Abbot, 1972

Southgate, G. W. *English Economic History*, Dent, London, 1962

Sutherland, D. *Raise Your Glasses*, Macdonald, London, 1969

Thomas, J. *The Rise of the Staffordshire Potteries*, Adams & Dart, Bath, 1971

Turner, E. S. *Taking the Cure*, Michael Joseph, London, 1967

Williams-Wood, C. *Staffordshire Pot Lids & Their Potters*, Faber & Faber, London, 1972

Wills, G. *English Glass Bottles for the Collector*, John Bartholemew, Edinburgh, 1974

Wills, G. *The Bottle Collector's Guide*, John Bartholemew, Edinburgh, 1977

INDEX